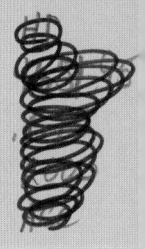

CHAIRMAN
OF THE
BOARD

A BIOGRAPHY OF CARL A. GERSTACKER

E. N. Brandt

Michigan State University Press • *East Lansing*

Copyright © 2003 by Michigan State University Press

∞ The paper used in this publication meets the minimum requirements
of ANSI/NISO Z39.48-1992 (R 1997) (Permanence of Paper).

Michigan State University Press
East Lansing, Michigan 48823-5245

Printed and bound in the United States of America.

09 08 07 06 05 04 03   1 2 3 4 5 6 7 8 9 10

LIBRARY OF CONGRESS CATALOGING-IN-PUBLICATION DATA
Brandt, E. N.
Chairman of the board : a biography of Carl A. Gerstacker / E.N. Brandt.
p. cm.
Includes bibliographical references and index.
ISBN 0-87013-683-6 (alk. paper)
1. Gerstacker, Carl A., 1916– 2. Dow Chemical Company. 3. Businessmen—
United States—Biography. 4. Chemical industry—United States—History.
I. Gerstacker, Carl A., 1916– II. Title.
HD9651.95B73 2003
338.7'66'0092—dc21
2003007815

Cover and book design by Sharp Des!gns, Lansing, MI

Visit Michigan State University Press on the World Wide Web at:
www.msupress.msu.edu

For Carl,
In memory of thirty-five years of
Working and playing together
As colleagues and friends

CONTENTS

Sources and Acknowledgments

I began to work closely with Carl Gerstacker in 1960, at about the time he became chairman of the board of Dow Chemical. He was taking on a heavy load of public speaking at the time and looking for someone to help draft his speeches. I was one of those given a tryout, and the two of us hit it off from the beginning. Soon I was called to his office every time he took on a major speech. At the beginning of our relationship, I was public relations manager of the Midland Division of the company (later called the Michigan Division). I then became assistant director of public relations for the parent firm, and later corporate public relations director. Over this period I was called to his office more and more often; and over time, the speech-writing tasks began to dwarf my duties with the public relations department. In fact, during the Vietnam War and the napalm protests against the Dow Company (from about late 1966 to roughly 1970), I found myself working (in all modesty) evenings and weekends trying to keep up with it all.

Meanwhile Carl and I were seeing more and more of each other socially, became golfing companions, and increasingly, traveling companions as well. Eventually we came to a point where he needed a full-time speech-writer-cum-assistant and I was relieved of most of my duties in the Public Relations department. "What title do you want?" Carl asked me. I said I had a friend who did approximately the same thing at General Electric, and his title was "assistant to the chairman." "We don't have any 'assistant to the' people at Dow," Carl said. "Things change too often. Pick out a title you like over the weekend and let me know what it is."

The following Monday my title became "Director of Business Communications" for the company, and that remained my title for a long time. The relationship with the chairman was a good deal more important than the title. On weekends I was his chain-sawing buddy. He gave me a key to his retreat at Wixom Lake, and we met there often, sometimes for business, sometimes for pleasure, most of the time for a mixture of both. From 1969 on, I was also involved with the Gerstacker Foundation; and in 1980, became a trustee and its secretary. Carl and I worked together on many of the projects and organizations described in the pages that follow.

It never occurred to me, in all those years, that I might one day be called upon to write his biography. It never even occurred to me that he could die, for that matter, but he did. It hurt me terribly when he told me, a few weeks before the end, that he did not want me to come by any more—I might be carrying the germs that would kill him.

Over those approximately thirty-five years, I learned more about him and his family and his problems and his accomplishments than most biographers, I suspect, ever know about their subjects, or at least as much. I had gone with him to see his first wife, for example, when she was confined to a mental institution (of course, I stayed in the car). I had gone to

his daughter Lisa's wedding. We had gone snorkeling together off the coast of St. John in the Virgin Islands. And, we had gone together to the little black church that he attended on St. John, where he was usually asked to read the scripture lesson. He tried to teach me to play tennis several times, but it did not work. As it turned out, almost everything else did. In brief, I worked and played with this man, in total confidence and intimacy, for some thirty-five years.

He gave most of his business papers and records to the Post Street Archives long before he died. These included materials about those aspects of his life about which I knew little or nothing. His letters to the folks back home during his six years in the military during World War II, for example, enabled me to reconstruct his military career. Similarly, his college letters, which his mother had kept, provided valuable insights on his college career.

I also had the assistance of a reading committee, which consisted of H. D. (Ted) Doan, his close friend and longtime colleague at Dow; Esther Schuette Gerstacker, his widow; Lisa J. Gerstacker, his daughter; Gail Allen Lanphear, his niece; Alan W. Ott, longtime chairman of the Chemical Bank in Midland and another close friend; and William D. Schuette, his stepson. I am immensely grateful for their understanding, help, and counsel in the process of writing this book.

In addition, there were a number of close relatives and friends with whom I conducted special interviews. These included the six persons listed above plus Alexio R. Baum, stepgrandson; Bette M. Gerstacker, daughter; Sandra Schuette Joys, stepdaughter; Myles Martel, speech coach; the Rev. Wallace H. Mayton III; Paul F. Oreffice and Frank P. Popoff, former presidents and CEOs of Dow; Gretchen Schuette, stepdaughter; and John Zimmerman, director of the Midland United Way organization. I extend my grateful appreciation to all of them.

I also enjoyed the advantage of access to the Dow Oral History Program, an oral history program which now contains extensive oral history interviews with more than 150 Dow executives, inventors, and other historic figures. Those consulted in the process of compiling this biography are listed as appendix A in this book.

The Carl A. Gerstacker Papers and the Dow Oral History series are housed at the Post Street Archives, which I was privileged to use as an office. The bulk of the materials for the book were thus readily available at all times, an enormous advantage for any author. I am especially indebted to Kathy Thomas of the Archives for her patient and uncomplaining help when I had problems of various sorts. I also was given access to the papers and records of the foundations of which Carl was such an integral part—the Elsa U. Pardee, Rollin M. Gerstacker, and Midland Area Community Foundations. I am especially grateful to Mary F. McDonough, of the Gerstacker Foundation, for assistance of many kinds in this connection.

For those materials not ready to hand, I had the willing cooperation of various other persons and organizations. Susan E. Lobsinger of Central Michigan University provided material concerning Gerstacker's first honorary doctorate, conferred by that school in 1957. Dr. Peter Mitchell of Albion College, and Jennifer Thomas, college archivist, provided excellent materials concerning his long, warm relationship with Albion. Sandra Schuette Joys furnished copies of various materials concerning the "Picnic in the Redwoods." The Council of Michigan Foundations kindly provided a videotape of Carl and Esther Gerstacker being interviewed on the subject of philanthropy by Prof. Philip Mason of Wayne State University in 1991. Alan W. Ott provided access to a number of vital materials, ranging from Carl's birth certificate to his death certificate, most notably a copy of the voluminous U.S. Estate Tax Return filed on his behalf.

Esther Gerstacker graciously provided full access to her photographic collection, and loaned the bulk of those included in the photo section. Most of the other photos came from the Post Street Archives. Others were provided by Bette and Lisa Gerstacker, and by the Rollin M. Gerstacker Foundation.

Throughout the work on this volume I have had the support and comfort of a loving wife, and that means more than I can say.

Since I have been provided all these privileges and boons, you will understand why I consider myself a very lucky fellow, not the least of my many blessings having been those many years of close association with a truly remarkable man. I can only hope that I have dealt with a wealth of material in the competent fashion it merits.

E. N. BRANDT
Midland, Michigan
December 30, 2002

INTRODUCTION

M OST OF THE TIME THE CARD GAME TOOK PLACE AFTER the dishes had been cleared away, but sometimes they played before the meal, at Carl's house. It did not make a lot of difference to Carl Gerstacker. He would always suggest a game that would be suitable for the group assembled, depending on how many people were going to play, and the ages of those people. Anyone beyond babyhood was eligible, and emergence from babyhood in his book was determined by the ability to sit at a table, hold a fistful of cards, and lay them politely on the table.

His fund of games was inexhaustible. He had traveled all over the world collecting them, and he brought them back to Michigan. He knew games that were easy for small children, games that were suitable for adults, games suitable for adults who seldom played cards, and games for a mix of adults and children, which was most often the case around his table. At the start of the game, if one or more of the participants had never played the game, he would review the rules and the scoring and permit a practice hand or two

One of the inviolable rules of these games was that he was the scorekeeper. He would keep the score with a stub of a pencil on a piece of scrap paper. After each hand or two he announced the score aloud, for each player, indicating who was leading and who was behind, always announcing his score last, referring to himself as "Old White Hat."

The name came from the cowboy books and movies that he enjoyed in which the hero always wore a white hat and the bad men always wore black ones. If "Old White Hat" was winning the game (and he usually was), it was even more enjoyable for him.

His colleagues at the company where he worked, where he was chairman of the board, said knowingly to each other, "Gerstacker needs to be in control" (which was true). They also said to each other, just as knowingly, "Gerstacker will tell you what the rules are" (and that was true, too).

The younger generation, looking back on these games, said, "He taught us about winning and losing," and "He made sure you understood that you had to play by the rules, and that everybody had to play by the rules."

"All lessons aren't necessarily verbal," one of them said.

After he died, what his children and grandchildren and stepchildren and stepgrandchildren remembered most vividly about him were those card games. They did not know about his accomplishments as a business leader, board chairman, financier, and philanthropist. They knew him as a crafty competitor at dirty sevens, crazy eights, hearts, kings-in-the-corners, two-handed rummy and two-on-two rum, bridge, golf (the card game), three-handed bridge, go-rum, old maid, several kinds of poker, and a variety of other games.

As he lay in his coffin at the funeral parlor, in April of 1995, there was much whispering and consulting among the young folks, and passing back and forth of playing cards. And when the coffin was closed the final time on his mortal body there had been tucked into his breast pocket a handful of playing cards—the heart suit was the one they had chosen, all thirteen cards of that suit. Each of the children—thirteen of them participated—had scrawled a little message on one of the cards, such as "We love you, Grampa," and then they slipped the cards into the coffin.

They put the rest of the deck into the coffin as well. "One of the really basic rules was that you didn't play with a partial deck," one of them said. "He would have been really upset without a full deck."

"Old White Hat," as he styled himself, would have been so very pleased that he had been a successful teacher, a vocation that brought him much pleasure.

This is the story of "Old White Hat," and also of the Chairman of the Board. That is how most of the outside world knew him.

1

Rollie and Eda, 1916–34

1916 Born Carl Allan Gerstacker on 6 August in Cleveland, Ohio, second child and first son of Rollin Michael Gerstacker and Eda Uhinck Gerstacker. Rollin ("Rollie") is a mechanical engineering graduate of Case Institute of Technology in Cleveland and spends his entire career in the engineering firm of Bartlett & Snow there. Eda is one of identical twins, Eda and Elsa, born to a local farming family. Rollie and Eda meet as classmates at West High School, Cleveland.

1921 Begins kindergarten at Landon Elementary School, Cleveland. Rather sickly as a child, misses one semester entirely. He and sister Elsa, four and one-half years older, begin spending summers in Midland, Michigan, with their uncle and aunt, James T. Pardee and Elsa Uhinck Pardee. (Pardee, a class-mate, close friend, and early financial backer of Herbert H. Dow, founder of the Dow Chemical Company, will become board chairman of Dow Chemical in 1935).

1930 Enters West High School, Cleveland. Delivers newspapers for spending money. When he is thirteen, he and his father study stock market and he begins investing his earnings from paper route. Plays tennis, golf, ping pong, softball, and other sports. Editor of school paper, *The West Higher.*

1934 Graduates from high school in January as class salutatorian and as such gives first public address, entitled "Two Wars and Two Debts."

ARL'S STORY BEGINS WITH ROLLIE AND EDA. THEY FIRST
met as classmates at West High School in Cleveland.
Rollie was one of the brightest lads in the class, the
son of Michael Gerstacker, the druggist who owned Gerstacker's Drugstore over on Fulton Street, on Cleveland's west
side. Rollie worked there after school. Eda was something of
a celebrity around the school, one of a set of identical twins,
Eda and Elsa, the daughters of a farming couple, the Uhincks.
They dressed identically most of the time, and resembled
each other so closely that no one could tell them apart except
their mother, and sometimes even she was not sure. They
came to West High after completing grade school in a one-
room schoolhouse in the farming area of south Cleveland.

Cleveland's south side was populated mostly by Germans
in those days, and most of the Germans were farmers.
The Gerstacker family came to the United States from
Bavaria, from a village called Kirchensittenbach, not far from
Nuremberg. Their farming background was betrayed by the
very name—Gerstacker, in German, means "barley field."
Rollie's grandfather, the first of the family to arrive, got a job
working on a railroad-building crew when he came to the
United States, and was especially remembered for his thrifti-
ness, which was inherited by Rollie. Rollie's father Michael
worked as a stevedore in Cleveland for awhile, and then bor-
rowed money to go to Philadelphia to study pharmacy.

Michael spent his entire working career in the Fulton
Street drugstore that he bought upon returning to Cleveland;
late in his career, however, he went out of business when a
chain drugstore bought land neighboring his store and he
chose not to compete with it.

The Uhinck girls decided very early on that they did not
want to follow old-country tradition and marry one of the
German farm boys in their neighborhood and raise lots of
children, as their family more or less expected them to do.

3

They had higher ambitions, and decided they would go to college and become schoolteachers—which both of them did.

Rollie also decided to go on to college, and enrolled in mechanical engineering at Case Institute of Technology, in downtown Cleveland, in due time graduating with a degree in engineering.

He worked at several jobs around Cleveland, and finally settled in at the Bartlett & Snow engineering and construction firm, where he spent his career. Bartlett & Snow specialized in ore-handling machinery for the boats that plied the Great Lakes. In addition to making and installing this kind of machinery, the firm also built sewage disposal plants. Eventually Rollie was in charge of a group of engineers for the firm.

It would be romantic to say that Eda and Rollie were high school sweethearts in the good old American tradition, but they were just good friends who enjoyed each other's company and always got along well. Both seem to have been waiting for someone else, who never came along. When they had a little more experience in life, and were twenty-five years old, they decided to marry.

It turned out to be a very solid marriage. Their first child, whom Eda named Elsa for her twin sister, arrived in February of 1912. Eda then gave up her teaching job and became a full-time housewife. Carl was born in August 1916, which completed the family. As he looked back on his family situation years later, Carl said that "the more people I meet the more I realize that our family (1) has more money than the great majority, (2) is happier than most, and (3) is like the majority of people, who are really good solid Americans."[1]

When he was five he entered the kindergarten class at Landon Elementary School, whose principal had been Eda Gerstacker's teacher in that one-room school in south Cleveland. "That was awful," Carl said, "because the principal knew

me from day one. My older sister had excelled at languages and I had a cousin who excelled in math and science. Every time I got to a class the teacher would say, 'Are you that long German name? Are you related to so and so?'"

One of his earliest memories was of a neighbor lady "who got annoyed with me and threatened to cut my head off with a butcher knife when I was probably about three. I was so frightened that I had an accident in my pants on the way home. When I explained what had happened to my mother, she was furious, but she would not say anything bad about the lady! She finally said, 'The lady was a fine swimmer.' She always tried to concentrate on something good. She believed that you should never say anything ill about anybody."[2]

He also remembered his mother saying to him, "Carl, you're as good as anyone in the world, but you're not better than anyone else." "I used to think she had slipped up somewhere in that," he said, "it didn't make complete sense to me. I gradually began to understand that she meant that you could be anything in the world you wanted to be if you were willing to try hard enough and that you should never look down on anyone else or feel that you were better than anyone else. It is a great principle."

She also taught him not to get into a fight unless he expected to win it. "She thought parents should not fight the battles of their kids," he said. "I remember vividly being beaten up by another kid in a neighborhood fight. I used to get into lots of fights. I remember out of the corner of my eye seeing that she was watching out of the window, but she never did anything to break up the fight. That was my problem, in her opinion. If I got beaten up, I would just do better the next time, which was a good feeling to have."

The fact that he was an only son was a major factor, he thought. "I often think mothers are never completely satisfied with their own fathers or with their husbands," he said. "If

5

they have a male child, mothers are determined to program that child to have the best qualities of their own father and the best qualities of their husband, without the qualities of which they are not so fond. They work very hard at doing that. They are never completely successful, but since they have tried so hard, they tend to have a great love for an only male child. My present wife has the same feeling about her only male child."[3]

They lived on West 102nd Street, not too far from the lake (Lake Erie), just south of Clifton Boulevard, and only half a block away from the Pardees, who lived in a big house on Clifton. From his earliest days he knew them as "Unkie"— Uncle Jim—and Aunty, his mother's twin sister. The Pardees also had a "summer place" up in Midland, Michigan—it was a comfortable old farmhouse on Main Street, just up the street from Uncle Jim's old friend Herbert Dow—and as the years went on the Pardees spent more and more of their time there.

From the time he was five, little Carl and his sister Elsa spent most of their summers up in Midland with Unkie and Aunty. It was like having a second set of parents, he said. Some of his earliest financial training came from those days with Unkie and Aunty, too. Uncle Jim "loved to educate me in various ways," he said.

> For example, he paid me to pick up the fallen apples from the apple trees in his yard. For a cherry basket full I got one penny. I began to negotiate with him. When the apples were big, it didn't take much to fill a cherry basket, but when they were tiny little apples I had to work awfully hard. I remember really bargaining with him and his laughing, I'm sure, on the side, and finally giving in to me. We had a lot of negotiations on things like that, which I later found were very educational. The two of them, my father and Mr. Pardee, were a great influence on me that way.[4]

6

Pardee loved to have the children get up early and have breakfast with him before he went off to work, but the children, being "on vacation," preferred to sleep in. So Uncle Jim would put a dime under their breakfast plates, and if they got up in time they got the dime. If they were not up by the time he left he pocketed the dimes and went on down to the office.

The Pardees saw a great deal of the Dows socially during these times, and Carl grew up knowing the Dow family on a first-name basis. He did not get to know Herbert Dow himself very well, but he did have one memorable session playing checkers with the man. "At the time I thought I was a very good checkers player," Carl said.

H. H. Dow *was* a very good checkers player. He used to play with the hourly people in the plant. I remember clearly one Sunday afternoon visiting the Dow home on Main Street. I must have mentioned checkers, being a brash young kid, so he offered to play with me. I remember it vividly because he beat me once rather badly and then he beat me again. I remember thinking I was just a little kid and this grown man would throw me a game somewhere along the way. But no way, he just clobbered me, game after game! I never thought I was a good checkers player after that.

When he reached high school age, he went to West High School as his parents had; it was the principal college preparatory choice in Cleveland. When he looked back on his high school days his most vivid memories were of the toughest teachers at West High:

. . . the ones who gave me a lot of homework and tough grades. Those are the ones everyone remembers. I remember the first day of the World Series when a few of us wanted to listen to it on the radio. We went to our home room teacher and said

7

we wanted to be excused to go because we wanted to listen to the baseball game. She thought that was absolutely ridiculous and said "No." So we went to the assistant principal. He thought it was humorous that we would try that hard, so he said, "Yes." That was a great lesson to me that you should never take the first "no." Often if you keep trying, you will find someone who will agree to do what you want, even if the first answer was "no."

He was quite sickly as a child, seeming to have more sniffles and sneezes and flu bugs than any of his school friends, but his mother was a model of patience and did not mind at all serving as his nurse. The usual childhood diseases hit him very hard and kept him out of school for varying periods of time. Once he was absent the greater part of a semester and had to stay behind his class, much to his chagrin. "My mother was a member of a women's study club, the Clytean Club," he recalled many years later, "and when I had to stay home from school my mother used me as a captive audience, as I lay on my sick bed, to practice the talks she had to give at her club. I had to learn all about Lake Titicaca, and how to pronounce long words like Ixtacihuatl and Popocatepetl. I learned more as a captive audience for my mother's Clytean Club papers, that has actually helped me in my business life, than I learned in most of my courses as a chemical engineer at the University of Michigan."[5]

In Latin class, which he did not like, he developed a habit of writing out the translations in the book.

We were allowed to look things up in the back of the book, and as the teacher walked around the class I would always be looking things up in the back of the book so she couldn't see that I had cheated by writing the translations in the front. But she

wasn't born yesterday! One day while she was walking around she stopped at my place, and she stayed and stayed. I fumbled at the back and I fumbled and fumbled and fumbled, and finally she began to laugh because she knew what I had done. She had seen kids before! She said, "The only way you can get out of this is to be Cicero in the Latin play, and if you do that I will forget the cheating." I ended up being Cicero in a Latin play and probably learned more Latin than I would have learned in a long time.

He delivered newspapers while he was in high school to earn himself a little pocket money, but he spent hardly any of it and it began to accumulate; he talked to his father, who followed the stock market daily, looking for advice on where to invest it. "You ought to buy some common stock in a company," his father said.

This was 1930, and Carl was thirteen. "I didn't know what he was talking about," he said.

He explained that there had been a big crash in the stock market and that it would therefore be a wonderful time to invest . He wanted me to withdraw all my savings from my paper routes and other jobs, and I had some government bonds. (The total, he told a reporter many years later, was about $1,000.) I said, "Okay, what should I buy?" He said I ought to buy Dow Chemical stock, since it was way down to $75 a share. We took all my life savings and bought Dow Chemical stock at $75 a share. A few months later he said we had to talk some more because that stock was now down to $50 a share. He said, "I feel pretty bad that you've lost a third of your money. I really don't have much money, but I have just enough to invest the same amount as you did and buy more shares at $50 each than you

9

bought at $75 each, so I'll trade you $50 shares for $75 shares."
I said, "Okay." My $50 a share stock, adjusted for splits, has an
adjusted cost basis of 27 cents a share today,

he said, in 1988.

The stock market became the principal subject of discussion between the father and son, and their correspondence
was full of such discussions until his father's death in 1945. "I
think the greatest experience of all was my father having me
gamble all of my assets on one thing," he said. "Very few people go through an experience like that. You can go to school
and play with things, but when it's your paper route and
you've saved your money and you've given up and sacrificed
buying things you wanted, you *care* and you pay attention."

Unfortunately his father was not a happy man, he admitted.

10

My father did not like his boss and he did not like the company
he worked for. He would talk about this at dinner time, and it
dawned on me that because he was anxious for my sister and me
to have an education, he was trapped in a situation that was very
distasteful to him. He couldn't quit because he needed the
money and there were no other jobs. That situation impressed
me greatly. I wanted never to be in a position where I couldn't
tell my boss to go to hell or quit the company for which I worked.
I never wanted to be in economic trouble. I wanted to be inde-
pendent so that I never had to be as unhappy as my father was
with his daily work. That was very strong in my feeling.

Although he was a mechanical engineer, what his father
really loved was finance and investment, Carl said.

During the 1930s Depression, he subscribed to advisory services. We would read the magazines and talk in the evening
about what stock would be a good investment. We made every

mistake anybody could make, but we did it with very small amounts of money. He taught me more than any college course. My father and I made all the mistakes you can make, but I learned more things from that work with my father.

One evening, he said to me, "City Service Oil is selling at seven-eighths of a dollar. Think of that. It can't go down very far because it is less than a dollar now. If it went up to five or ten, think of the money we would make. What an opportunity." We bought City Service and it dropped from seven-eighths to three-quarters to one half to one quarter. Finally, they gave us one share for twenty. We felt like we had been raped because although we knew you could split, we had never heard of a reverse split. I learned that it didn't matter what you paid for anything, whether you paid a dollar or ten thousand dollars, it could go up or down the same way, and that being low-priced meant nothing.

When Republic Steel had a sit-down strike, one of the very early sit-down strikes in Cleveland, I thought it was terrible that the workers were taking over the company. I bought a few shares of Republic Steel stock to show my confidence in the management. I lost money on that deal. I also learned that you should never invest out of emotion. You can write them a nice letter and say, "I'm for you and I like you," but don't put your money in.

11

When he came to the end of his high school days he learned another lesson. It had to do with discrimination. "I was the class salutatorian, but only because we had a rule that the valedictorian and salutatorian had to be of opposite sexes. Otherwise, two girls would have been valedictorian and salutatorian. I was merely the highest male." As salutatorian he had to give an address at the commencement exercises, and he carefully considered what he might talk about. He had never given a big public speech before.

I had read a book on the fact that the French had not paid their World War I debts. If we added up the interest and divided what they owed us among all the people, every man, woman and child in the United States, we all would have the money we needed in the 1930s Depression. That really bugged me, so I decided that this would be the subject of my commencement address. When I told my parents, they said, "You can't give a commencement address about why the French haven't paid their World War I debts." I said, "It's my speech." Again I went to the high school principal or assistant principal who said, "Sure, go ahead." Obviously, he knew no one paid attention to commencement addresses. I gave a wonderful commencement address about why the French had not paid their debts.

Although he was to give literally thousands of speeches in his life, that first one, entitled "Two Wars and Two Debts," always remained one of his favorites. It began "Shylocks! Money grubbers! War profiteers! Does no one of you arise to these appellations? You should, for these epithets are typical of the average Frenchman's opinion of us. . . ."

The commencement ceremonies took place at the staid old Music Hall in downtown Cleveland in a gorgeous, big auditorium with a mammoth stage. "I had to memorize my speech," he said, "I remember that just before I got up, I saw all those people out there and I couldn't even remember my own name. When it was my turn, I couldn't think of anything at all at first, but I finally got going and got through it. It's a great speech."[6]

One of the best business speakers of his day was on his way.

DUMBBELL, 1934–39

1934 On 5 February begins work at Dow Chemical in Midland as a seventeen-year-old laboratory helper, working thirty-nine hours per week at thirty-five cents per hour.

Enters a competitive exam, the winners of which earn entry to the company's Student Training Course, and comes in first against mainly college graduates. He then commences a forty-two-week course, which involves seven weeks' work in six different Dow departments, moving through Physics Lab, Machine Shop, Main Lab, Pipe Shop, and Boiler Shop.

On 8 September enters the University of Michigan as a student in chemical engineering, having been told that Dow employs mostly chemists and chemical engineers. Joins Theta Xi social fraternity. Writes, principally sports, for *Michigan Daily*. Participates in golf, tennis, and softball.

1935 Returns to Dow for summer. Completes Student Training Course with stage in Electric Shop.

14

1936 In June serves as best man at wedding of his sister, Elsa, in Oberlin, Ohio, to William W. Allen of Dow's Agricultural Chemicals Department. Is tapped for Triangle, junior engineering honorary.

1937 Works at Dow fourth summer in a row. Is inducted into Scabbard and Blade Honorary Society. Is president of Theta Xi chapter.

1938 Graduates in June with bachelor of science degree in chemical engineering. Begins permanent work at Dow on 1 August after taking his parents on a vacation to California by automobile. In November is assigned to the accounting and auditing staff of Dowell, Dow's oil well servicing subsidiary.

1939 Doing detail accounting work, which he does not like at all, seriously contemplates leaving Dow. Tries unsuccessfully to get transferred to the financial side of the company.

DOW IS HIRING PEOPLE UP IN MIDLAND," UNCLE JIM told him in the course of his high school graduation festivities, "and you may be able to get a job." Such an opportunity was as rare as hen's teeth during the Depression years, so a few days later he hopped on an all-day bus from Cleveland to Midland to try his luck. It was good. On 5 February 1934, at the age of seventeen, he was hired on as an hourly laboratory helper in the Physics Research Laboratory, and appeared on the Dow payroll for the first time. He worked there for seven months that first time, until it was time to begin the fall semester at the University of Michigan, and that set a pattern for his college career—working every summer at Dow, earning money to supplement what his father was able to send him.

His first boss at Dow, when he was seventeen, was "a horrible boss," he remembered. "He constantly told me how dumb I was. He would give me jobs to do and not tell me how to do them. I would do them wrong and then he would tell me again how dumb I was."

This boss was Walter E. Roush, then a twenty-six-year-old research chemist looking ahead to a highly successful career at Dow. (Carl Gerstacker always refused to divulge his name, just like his mother not wanting to say anything bad about a person.) Roush, who had lost the sight in one eye in a lab accident (which gave him a permanent scowl), was an outspoken curmudgeon who freely vented his likes and dislikes all his life. He spent his later career as a senior research executive in Texas, where he was known affectionately to his younger colleagues as "Papa" Roush, and finished his career as chief of Dow Technology Centers worldwide. A chemist at Dow could hardly ask for a finer career, and his opinion that Gerstacker was a dumbbell made the young man miserable.

"My boss (Walt Roush) had a long talk with me this afternoon about the future, etc.," he wrote his parents. "He said

15

that I was probably the dumbest fellow he'd ever seen in the place. He said he thought, though, that I had some natural intelligence and might someday learn something. He says I do things without looking ahead and that I don't know how to use my hands."[1]

The Dow Chemical Company in those years had a very popular Student Training Course. It was designed for two purposes: to give incoming trainees, fresh out of college, some experience in the various basic work activities of the company; and to measure their aptitude for such types of work. The program lasted forty-two weeks and consisted of a seven-week stint in each of six different Dow departments—the Physics Lab, Machine Shop, Main Lab, Pipe Shop, Boiler Shop, and Electric Shop. The trainee was required to keep careful daily notes on his experiences in these places and was expected to spend two hours a day just bringing his notebook up to date. He was given grades on this notebook, and on his general performance, every seven weeks. The program was aimed at getting young recruits into the line of work to which they were most suited and in which they were most likely to succeed. It was one of the most successful programs the Dow company ever offered, producing an entire generation of the corporation's leaders.

At the beginning of 1934 the company had decided it would put eighteen young men through the program that year, but more than thirty employees had already applied for it, posing a ticklish question—which applicants to accept, and which to reject. At the suggestion of Steve Starks (the manager in charge of hiring and employee training), the company decided to give an intelligence exam, open to any employee who wished to apply for the program, and the eighteen scoring highest on this test would win the coveted places in the 1934 Student Training Course.

Carl Gerstacker asked if he could take the test too. Roush

16

told him not to bother. "You'd just be wasting your time because you're so dumb," Roush told him. "There's just no point in your taking the time." Gerstacker decided to take the exam anyway, even though the average age of the candidates was twenty-two (he was seventeen) and most were college graduates.

"About thirty of us took the exam, and it took three hours," he wrote home. "It was *tough*. They made this year's exam much longer, adding a lot of questions on mechanics, tools, etc. (I did very poorly on that part)."

He did not hear immediately from Roush how he had done on the test, so he went to Roush's boss, Dr. John J. Grebe, director of the Physics Lab, and asked him about it. Grebe "said he would tell me if it wouldn't make me too swell-headed," he wrote home. "The most wonderful thing happened," Grebe told him. "You came in first of all the people who took the exam." Since Grebe had heard from Roush how terrible and hopeless the young Gerstacker was, he was just delighted. He wrote his parents: "Mr. Grebe said he thought it would be a good thing for me to start in the Main and Physics labs because I have very little mechanical knowledge and they would probably think I was a 'dude' if I started in the Boiler Shop knowing as little as I do about tools, etc."

In the next few months he was counseled to take special courses in Boiler Shop operations at a night school operation in Bay City (he did not), and to acquire other shop skills (he did not), but he learned more about the basic operations of the Dow company in that period of time than he otherwise would have over the course of several years.

The trainees were graded on quality and quantity of work, general ability, personal cleanliness, response to orders, promptness, dependability, general deportment, and initiative. For his seven-weeks work in the Machine Shop, for example, Gerstacker was pleased to learn that he received the highest grades of the three trainees then going through

17

that shop (he had a grade of 93.5, and the other two trainees had 93), and he received a high grade on his notebook for the period (95), but was upset to learn that he had received the lowest grade of the three in dependability and general deportment.

"I tried my best to find out why I was the lowest of the three of us in Dependability but couldn't find out," he wrote home. "The only thing I can recall is making a box wrong in the Tin Shop and having to do it over again," he wrote home. The other two trainees were Lawrence ("Blackie") Blackhurst, who was then twenty-four, and Joe Glesner, nineteen.[2]

Much of what he had to do during this training period was rather menial work. Years later he remembered two of the roughest jobs he had to do. One involved ceramic valves. "They would wear from corrosive chemicals and somebody had to save them by putting a compound on them and grinding them so they would fit again," he remembered. "For one week all I did was grind plug cap valves by hand at a bench to make them fit. That job made me determined to get a college education," he laughed. "If I had to spend the rest of my life grinding plug cap valves, I'd go out of my mind!"

The other "worst job" he remembered was "when they had me down in the bowels of a building throwing out old time cards. They saved the time cards and after a while the time cards were overflowing so they wanted to throw out an early year or two. My job was to go through those cards and throw out this early year. For a couple of weeks, all by myself down in the basement someplace, all I did was root around and throw out old time cards. Again I thought, 'There's got to be a better way in this world!'"[3]

It was during this period that he began to develop some of the eccentric eating habits for which he was later noted. "I was making about $15 a week on a forty-hour week," he said.

"I was paying $5 for my room, so I didn't have much left over. I insisted on saving some money, so my dinner every night was two quarts of milk and a candy bar. I couldn't down the two quarts of milk without having the candy bar to help doll it up a little. That was the cheapest way I could eat, so I would sit in my room and drink two quarts of milk and eat a candy bar. But I was saving. I kept records of my expenditures and I was still saving money."

When the summer was over he headed for Ann Arbor and enrolled as a student in chemical engineering. He had been asking Uncle Jim and others what he ought to take in college, and the answers had come back virtually unanimous. "I went to all the Dow people and said, 'If I want to come back here to work, what should I take in college?' They laughed and said, 'We hire only scientists and engineers, so you have to take either science or engineering.' Chemical engineering seemed to combine both of these so I said I would take chemical engineering. I didn't like chemistry and I didn't like engineering, so I took chemical engineering."

19

The decision to go to Ann Arbor was his alone, for his father wanted him to follow in his own footsteps and go to Case Institute of Technology. "His only brother had gone there, as had my uncles and my cousin," Gerstacker said.

I was a little rebellious. I did not always want to do what others had done, so I wanted to go to some other place. My father almost got me to go to Case because at the last minute he said that he did not think I could graduate from Case and that I could not meet their academic standards. That almost got me there, but not quite, so I went to the University of Michigan. The Cleveland public schools were so good at that time that the chemical engineering department of the University of Michigan gave me eight hours advanced credit for which I had not even asked.

Taking a lot of courses he did not like proved to be "tough," he said.

> The University of Michigan prided itself on having a good chemical engineering department and on flunking out a lot of people. It was tough because I didn't like the course I was taking all that well. I also got involved in a lot of extracurricular things like writing for the newspaper and a lot of social things. I took my electives, not in chemistry or engineering, but in law for engineers and economics and things like that. In the beginning of my senior year, the head of the department called me in and said he wanted to have a heart-to-heart talk with me. He wasn't sure I had my heart in this whole thing and did I know that the taxpayers of the state of Michigan were subsidizing my education? I said that it had not occurred to me, so he told me how many dollars per year the taxpayers were paying for my education. He said that as far as he was concerned, they were not getting their money's worth. They were casting the seeds of learning on barren sands in my case, and that was terrible. That made me mad, so I ended up with all A's in my senior year. It was probably good for me.[4]

SHENANIGANS

In spite of his constant complaints that "I just work and work and still get lousy grades," Gerstacker seems to have enjoyed his college career to the fullest, and his good grades came rather easily. His father had sent his own golf clubs to Ann Arbor for his son to use, and Carl frequently played golf on the university course ("the University course is a swell course. It only costs 50 cents for 18 holes and has good greens and swell fairways. I wish Dad could come and play sometime"), and he also played tennis, softball, and Ping-Pong, and even horseshoes.[5]

20

In his freshman year he pledged the Theta Xi social fraternity, and was an active member of that fraternity for four
years, becoming chapter president in due course. He was not
good enough at tennis to make the varsity, but he still loved
tennis (one of the great loves of his life) and so he became
the tennis reporter for the *Michigan Daily*, the campus newspaper. "I'm still pretty darn busy," he wrote his parents in the
spring of 1936. "I am supposed to be playing on two softball
teams, a tennis team, and could probably play on a horseshoe
team although I am no good."

In the spring of 1936 he was "tapped" to be initiated into
Triangle, the junior engineering honorary. As one of only
thirteen so honored, he was introduced to the rather weird
shenanigans that then accompanied initiation into some of
the honorary societies. "Gosh we had a swell initiation yesterday," he wrote his parents.

We started out at about three o'clock. We all (eleven of us)   21
assembled in front of the library on roller skates with big dunce
caps on our heads. There was a big crowd of about 100 people
around watching. We had to get up on the grandstand and sing
and they threw buckets of cold water on us. I was delegated to
chase two dogs away and since I was on roller skates, I had quite
a time. Then they told me to go up and propose to one of the
girls watching the performance. She was quite nice looking so
it was kind of fun. She promised to marry me tomorrow. They
told me to go up and propose to some more so I started after a
bunch and they all ran away. "Goon child Gerstacker." We had
to race on roller skates and had a race running with a fellow on
our backs. Then we had to go and get a lot of gravel and spread
it on the walk through the engineering arch and get down on
our knees and scrub the walk with gravel and water and a scrub
brush. All the time we worked they kept pouring pails of cold
water on us. Then they took us inside, blindfolded us, and made

us form a chain gang on our knees and crawl all over the building and through all sorts of obstructions. My knees are ruined. We had a swell banquet afterward.

Monday night they came to "tap" us at 1:30 A.M., pulled me out of bed, rushed me outside, made me take off all my clothes, and made me roll around in the grass nude. One of the fellows in the house got some pictures of it and we really look like nudists. We had to go to school for two days with black triangles painted on our foreheads. . . . [6]

At the end of his sophomore year he was invited to be the best man at the wedding of his sister Elsa, then twenty-four. She was marrying William W. Allen, twenty-eight, who had embarked on a career with Dow Chemical five years before after graduating from the University of Minnesota. For most of his career, Bill would be manager of agricultural chemical sales for Dow. "Just what does a best man do anyway?" Carl wrote his mother. "What clothes should I bring home? Will we have to transport a lot of stuff to Oberlin [Ohio, where the wedding took place]? I had thought some of getting Bill and Elsa a car radio for their marriage etc. What do you think? I went over and priced Motorolas today and they want about $50 for a six tube set installed. If you can think of anything better, please suggest it."[7]

In his junior year he had his first serious girlfriend and began "going steady" with a coed named Edith. He described her to his father as

blond, 5' 4" fairly thin, blue eyes, pretty, sweet, smart, and so far I'm not in a position to judge her loving qualities, Pop. . . . Just got back from taking Edith to church. We went to the new Presbyterian church and I now feel very virtuous. . . . Friday night I took Edith to a party put on by the Triangles and Sphinxes (junior honoraries in both engine and lit. schools).

There was dancing, shuffle board, ping pong, and drinking downstairs and tobogganing out on the golf course. (We) went out tobogganing. We found a bunker that had about a five foot drop so we got everybody on the toboggan and I gave them a push and then hopped on the back. We went over the drop and Edith and I went flying up into the air. When I came down, I thought I was still on the toboggan but I wasn't. The rest of them were rapidly disappearing and I was bumping along on my seat. It's great fun this tobogganing.[8]

RELUCTANT ACCOUNTANT

In June 1938 he emerged from campus life into a "world gone mad," a world tottering on the brink of World War II, with Great Britain and France trying desperately to maintain the peace—"peace at any price," it was proclaimed—and Adolf Hitler, the madman German dictator, running amok across Europe. The United States, trying desperately to stay out of this conflict, was suffering an economic recession of sorts and the June graduates that year did not have an easy time finding employment.

23

"I was afraid I might not get a job with Dow because we had a mini-recession at that time," Gerstacker said. "Roosevelt kept trying to bring us out of the Depression and things would improve a little bit, but then we would go down again. Unfortunately, this was a bad time again. Very few of my class were getting jobs, and I wasn't either. I thought Dow would take me back again, but I wasn't sure. I was mighty happy when they said they had a job for me at $115 a month."

He seized the summer vacation as an opportunity to take his parents on a trip to the West Coast. "We drove out to California and back," he said. "I didn't go to commencement because you had to wait two weeks. Instead I took my parents

out west and then I immediately went to work at Dow."[9] It was a trip the Gerstacker family had been planning for and dreaming about for most of the time he had been away at school, and as it turned out it was to be his last extended time with his father. They visited Uncle Bob Uhinck, except that Uncle Bob had "Americanized" his name on arrival in California and was now known, with the rest of his family there, as "Ewing." Carl became fast friends with his first cousin, Helen Ewing. She was a giant of a woman who towered over him, and when they danced together they made a very odd couple indeed. They remained close friends throughout their lifetimes.

The Gerstackers also stopped in Oakland to visit the Pardee family (George C. Pardee was a first cousin of Uncle Jim), where they were entertained by Mrs. Helen Pardee and her daughters, Helen and Madeline. Cousin George had been governor of California in 1905 when the great San Francisco earthquake occurred; the family home has since become the Pardee Home Museum in downtown Oakland.

And then it was back to Midland and the job awaiting him at Dow. "The Dow people had told me that you had to take science or engineering," Gerstacker said later about his first full-time job at Dow.

> You had to have that kind of background, even if you were going to be a salesman or an accountant. I had struggled through that course and I was a chemical engineer. I came to Dow to work thinking that I would be in research or production. They said, "You are now an auditor with Dowell," which was a subsidiary. I hadn't taken a lot of accounting. I had taken all the electives I could, but here suddenly I was supposed to be an accountant. . . . That wasn't such a happy experience for me because it was real detail accounting and I never enjoyed

accounting or auditing that much. Here I was doing real detailed accounting and auditing.

His supervisor was Charles (Charlie) Penhaligen, a seasoned old veteran of the accounting field who had been working for a Midland bakery when Dow hired him. "He was a very exacting man," Gerstacker said. "His famous statement was, 'There's a right way and a wrong way to do everything. We're going to do it the right way because we only do it the right way. You don't show any individuality about accounting. It's either right or wrong.' He was a good, wonderful boss. He taught me a lot about accuracy."[10]

He was shown to his new workplace, which was in the basement, and found himself working alongside a nice young man with only a high school education. "He turned out more work than I did and this really bugged me," Gerstacker said. "So I began to cheat by going in at night. I didn't ring the time clock and I would work at night so that I could catch up and be better than this competitor. One night we found that we were both sneaking in to do more work at night!"

25

Since he was bored with accounting, he sought other work to do, and he decided to try remodeling the company's annual report. "The head of student training and hiring was Steve Starks, and I had met him off and on because I had come back and forth so many times," he said. "I didn't think much of Dow's annual report, and Steve also thought that our accounting was pretty stodgy. He encouraged me to redo the annual report, so I redid it in what I thought was a more modern, and more exciting and creative way. When it got to Willard Dow, the boss, he was furious! He was mad! I thought I had been set up because nobody else was willing to take the risk. I got in a little trouble trying to be more creative in the accounting, but I survived it."[11]

The annual report project was part of a quiet campaign to get out of the accounting end of the company and into the financial end, where his real interests lay. When that did not work he began to wonder whether he had made the right decision in going to Dow. "I was getting the feeling that people were being nice to me because of Mr. Pardee," he said, referring to his status as nephew of the chairman of the board.

> I thought I would never really find out whether I was good unless I went someplace where I wasn't known and where I didn't have a relationship with many of the people in the company. I was really torn. I was thinking of leaving, but not because I didn't like it. I loved it! I was really having a terrible internal struggle over this because I liked the fact that all my money was invested in the company and I didn't want to leave. But I felt I wasn't really being measured properly. Luckily I got into the Army where nobody knew me and I felt that maybe I could go through a period of understanding myself and feeling more self-confident.[12]

During his college career he had enrolled in the ROTC (Reserve Officer Training Corps) classes "because you got paid twenty cents a day and that seemed like a lot of money in those days. I really didn't care about the Army or the war or anything, but twenty cents a day was good stuff. When I graduated I was a second lieutenant in the reserves. I had made up my mind to resign as soon as I could, but you couldn't resign immediately."

He was about to pay for his reserve officer training with six years of active military duty.

3

TROUBLESHOOTER, 1940–46

1940   On 14 November becomes 32nd degree Mason at Bay City, Michigan, consistory.

As a reserve officer, writes asking if he is likely to be called to active duty. Is ordered to report for one year of duty, and is inducted into the U.S. Army as a second lieutenant on 11 December.

1941   In January is sent to Rock Island Arsenal, Iowa, for training as an army inspector of ordnance. Is then assigned to the Detroit Ordnance District, which sends him to a troubled Battle Creek, Michigan, firm, Duplex Printing Press Co., which has a contract to make 37 mm. gun carriages for the British but is going bankrupt. Reorganizes the firm's top management, and the firm earns an Army-Navy "E" Award a year later. Begins building a reputation as a crack troubleshooter for Army Ordnance.

In March, receives certificate of capacity for grade of first lieutenant. In April comes down with measles and is quarantined at Station Hospital, Ft. Custer, Michigan, returning to duty at end of month.

In August, now a first lieutenant, attends meeting of the Mobile Artillery Carriage Committee of the Ordnance Department, duty usually reserved for field-grade officers. On 28 October is promoted to chief of Artillery Division, Detroit Ordnance District, assuming responsibility for about 100 ordnance inspectors around Michigan.

1942   On 21 May is promoted to captain. On 4 June is called to Washington, D.C., where Ordnance Dept. is organizing manufacturers of the same or similar items for mutual assistance and exchange of information; is to be the officer working with manufacturers of 37 mm., 57 mm., 75 mm., and 3-inch mobile artillery carriages. Moves to Reading, Pennsylvania, on detached service from DOD, to work with companies scattered from Oklahoma to Maine.

1943   Is called to Washington again on 13 June and assigned as a key officer in production sector of carriage section of artillery branch, which is "in trouble." Subsequently spends much time in Washington.

On 25 September his father, who has been plagued with heart problems for many years, retires at age fifty-eight.

In November, anxious for overseas duty, is sent to Aberdeen Proving Ground, Maryland, to train for field duty, but his superiors refuse to release him for overseas duty.

In December, learns that his request for promotion (to major) is "going through."

1944   On 3 January his uncle, James T. Pardee, dies, and on 2 October his aunt, Elsa Uhinck Pardee, also dies, both following battles with cancer. Elsa, by the terms of her will, establishes the Elsa U. Pardee Foundation "for the promotion of the control and cure of cancer." He becomes a trustee and will remain active in the Pardee Foundation the remainder of his days. Substantial amounts of the Pardee fortune are also bequeathed to Eda Gerstacker and to her children, Carl and Elsa.

On 5 June is transferred to Ordnance Department, New York City office, and spends remainder of the war period riding herd on ordnance suppliers in the New York area.

29

1945   Rollin M. Gerstacker dies of heart disease in March at age sixty.

With the war ended, is assigned to the Arthur D. Little Co. in Boston "to teach them about artillery." A. D. Little has a contract to develop a plan for storage of World War II artillery in the event of another war, and he works on this project about six months.

1946   Is discharged from the U.S. Army as a major on 1 May. Returns immediately to Dow and is assigned to Production Engineering Department. On 26 August transfers to Purchasing Department as expeditor. Resumes efforts to move to financial sector.

S OMETIMES A MISTAKE CAN TURN OUT TO BE ONE OF THE best things you ever did, and that was the case with Gerstacker when World War II came along.

By the fall of 1940 he had saved enough money to buy an automobile, and yearned for the freedom it would give him to go where he wanted, when he wanted. Like everyone else he saw the war clouds gathering in Europe as Adolf Hitler invaded nation after nation, and he was a reserve officer subject to immediate call to arms if the United States got into the war. On the other hand, if he were called to duty, he didn't want a new car on his hands. So he wrote to the Detroit Ordnance District, to which he was assigned, asking if he were apt to be called up.

By way of response he received a telegram ordering him to report for one year of active duty, and on 11 December he was inducted into the army as a second lieutenant and reported to the Detroit Ordnance District for duty.[1]

30

"I was so naïve," he said years later, "I can't believe it. The Japanese have a saying, 'It's the nail that sticks up that gets hit on the head.' That's true of the army. They might have forgotten me."[2]

He reported to Detroit, and a colonel promptly announced: "You're going to be an artillery expert!" And so it came to be. They shipped him off to Rock Island Arsenal, Iowa, for training, and a few weeks later the newly minted artillery expert was sent to Battle Creek, Michigan, where Detroit had one of its toughest problems. This was the Duplex Printing Press Co., which had a contract to make 37 mm. gun carriages for the British forces but was floundering and close to bankruptcy.

The twenty-four-year-old lieutenant found himself the unquestioned boss of a major industrial concern overnight, but he was full of confidence. "I may be wrong but I think I'm on top of my job," he wrote home to "Mom & Dad" on 9

March. "It appears that I know more, at least about my job, than any of my civilians [his civilian assistants] do, and I am very definitely the boss as far as they and Duplex are concerned. Most of Duplex' plant heads are men they hired out of the auto industry—good men, with lots of experience. I sensed initially that they were doubtful of my youth, etc., but I think now that in most cases I have their respect. Strangely enough (I guess it isn't strange) the policy that Penhaligen pounded into me [Charlie Penhaligen, of Dow Accounting] of carefully and accurately analyzing everything has been most important."

The Duplex people found out immediately that Gerstacker might be only twenty-four years old, but was no pushover. He wrote home with this story.

> The treasurer came in and wanted me to approve an advance payment to a subcontractor of 25% of cost of a machine. Everything looked all right but I got out Duplex' purchase order and found that it was for quite a bit less than the amount of the advance payment indicated. I showed the discrepancy to the treasurer and he was surprised. He had missed it. He called in the purchasing agent and he too, did not know why the subcontractor was charging more than the purchase order called for. The local office of the subcontractor didn't know either and they finally had to contact the subcontractor's home office, where information developed that the extra charge was for some extra equipment. That deal should impress the treasurer and purchasing agent with the idea that I'm not a rubber stamp.[3]

31

Within a few days after arriving in Battle Creek and getting acquainted with the situation there, Gerstacker spotted what appeared to be the key to the problem—one of the company's top managers, a man referred to in his correspondence only as "Decker," was an alcoholic and was prone

to strange acts of management (or mismanagement) under the influence of liquor. Gerstacker called the man in and warned him that "for his own good he should change his ways."

The next morning Decker called in to the Duplex phone operator to say he had personal business and wouldn't be down till afternoon. Gerstacker was about to ask Detroit for the man's release (he was a civil service employee) when Decker called. Gerstacker asked him what was going on, and he said, not very coherently, that he "was discouraged and was going to South Bend and might be back Wednesday." Gerstacker knew that "you can get into trouble if you just fire a civil service man, so I tried to get him to say he was quitting. He was too canny for that but I worked him into admitting that he was 'wilfully neglecting his duty.' I immediately wrote Detroit the details insisting that I be allowed to fire him without further ado, and told the plant police not to let him back in the plant without telling me."

A few days later Decker showed up to "pack up his tools," and was sent to get a passout for them from Gerstacker. "He was pretty drunk," Gerstacker wrote home. "I still hadn't power to fire him but I talked him into signing a resignation. Some fun." He wrote to Mom and Dad, "Gosh but I love this job, the time just flies and there is never a dull moment. It's almost too good to be true."

The Duplex problem seems to have been a test case for the young lieutenant. He passed with flying colors. Duplex not only rebounded from the shadow of bankruptcy but a year later was awarded an Army-Navy "E" Award for excellence as a military supplier.

The Ordnance Department began to throw its tougher problems his way, and soon he was in a situation where he spent most of his time at the Detroit Ordnance District, then located in the big National Bank Building in downtown

32

Detroit, across the square from City Hall. He visited Battle Creek and the Duplex firm one or two days a week. He had bought the automobile he so badly wanted, a 1941 Ford coupe, and was commuting across the state, from Detroit to Battle Creek, much of the time. He called the car "Eda II" because, he said, it "did so much for him," just like his mother.

On fall weekends he could even get himself a date and take in the football games at Ann Arbor, which he greatly enjoyed.

One of the early military goals he had set for himself was "to make it to captain in less time than the four years it's supposed to take," and he made the first step in this climb, from second lieutenant to first lieutenant, in a matter of about six months. Making it to captain would take him another year.

By August, a seasoned veteran of eight months in the army, he was sent off to Camp Perry, Ohio, to attend a meeting of the Mobile Artillery Carriage Committee of the Ordnance Department. He welcomed this assignment for two reasons: first, because it was the type of duty usually reserved for field-grade officers (he was one of two junior officers to attend, and the sole representative of Detroit), and second, because it gave him a chance to visit his parents in Cleveland.

In September he submitted a request to be released at the end of his first year of service, which was due to end on 10 December, but it came back. His commanding officer, Lt. Col. R. Z. Crane, had written "Disapproved" on it. He settled down for a long stay in the army.

It was not all skittles and beer. We get a rare glimpse of his being called "on the carpet" from a letter to his parents of 12 October 1941. "It's something like this—," he wrote.

When I recommend something, they almost always approve it and their verbal attitude has been "Don't bother us with the minor things—use your own judgment and don't tell us about

33

them." I have always protected Duplex and me on the major things by written approval, but the countless minor differences I have settled. . . . It takes forever to get approval out of Detroit (months, in fact) and it has not yet been received although Duplex has had to go ahead and order before the changes are approved if they are to get any carriages built. Last Monday, I tried to point out this bottleneck to the Colonel but he "reversed the field" and bawled me out for some of the changes I had authorized. He said that I had no authority to accept anything not exactly to print and that he did not have the authority—only Washington could do it. I asked him whether he realized that we were constantly getting shipments of steel, for instance, that varied a little in chemicals or physicals from the requirements and that if Washington had to approve all those things that we would either have to maintain constant contact with Washington or practically stop making gun carriages.

(By the way, I should inject here the fact that the Proving Grounds and other Army agencies can find no fault with our product and they are probably the best carriages ever built in this country.) He said he was sorry but his hands were tied. This last week I have been following this policy to the letter and have made life miserable for Detroit. There are a number of things that must be approved immediately. I have Rock Island's approval and know they're all right anyway but can't get anything out of Detroit. They finally told me over the phone that I should tell Duplex to order material without the approval, but I said that was not fair to Duplex or me and was reversing their position that everything must be approved. I have them cornered and they know it, and I'm afraid they hate me for it.

At the crux of the situation, he said, is that

some big boy in Washington will not delegate any authority because he does not want to be responsible for the mistakes of

subordinates down the line. He wants the subordinates to use their good judgment, but if anything goes wrong, the subordinate was outside of his authority and is doubly the goat. Col. Crane is in the same position. He wants production and knows that I must make decisions on the spot to maintain production, but officially states that I can make no decisions. His entire life is the Army and he does not ever want to be put in a position where he can be made an example of, and perhaps be kicked out. On the other hand, my only interest is to give the country what it wants—the best guns as soon as possible. I don't care whether I'm the goat or not if I know that I've done the right thing.

He and Colonel Crane were absolutely deadlocked on this issue, which was fundamental to the whole program of the Department of Defense. "I may be fired before it's over, but I will at least have had my day in court," he wrote.[4]

Two weeks later, instead of being fired, he received his biggest promotion of the war. He was called in and informed that he was to move back to Detroit to take over his new duties as chief of the Artillery Division, Detroit Ordnance District.

CHIEF OF ARTILLERY DIVISION

Although he was still a first lieutenant, Gerstacker now had a considerable staff, including, he wrote his mother, a Harvard graduate who was his chief assistant, as well as about 25 office employees ("a number of whom are making more than I am," he observed), and about 100 ordnance inspectors stationed around the state.

His predecessor in the position "didn't have time to explain any of my duties to me, so I just jumped in with both feet and took over," he wrote home. "Things are in a great

35

muddle, in my opinion, and I'm trying hard to reorganize while keeping the business going at the same time."

All this was taking place just a few weeks before the Japanese attack on Pearl Harbor plunged the United States into the war, and privately at this time Gerstacker was very upset with the direction his country was taking. "I am very much depressed about our national affairs," he wrote his parents in October 1941.

> We are now paying for England's war and I feel that we will soon be fighting it for her. I've heard cases where our companies can't sell copper articles to South America because of priorities, but South America buys, with money loaned by us, copper from England that we gave England under Lend-Lease. I hear that we have to buy back from England copper for our Western power projects, copper we gave England. We're buying guns from Canada for cash and giving these or similar guns to England. If England ever intended to use her soldiers to attack Germany, she would do it now. The war can't be won without an invasion of the continent. Therefore it must be our soldiers who will do the invading. I have preached a stay-out policy since the war began. I have written my Congressman a number of times.

36

The net result of this thinking was that a few weeks before Pearl Harbor, he joined the America First Committee, the premier organization of the nation's isolationists. "I joined the America First Committee of Gen. R. E. Wood of Sears-Roebuck last week," he announced to Mom and Dad. "I sent them $5.00. Some people think them rather leftish but I believe that they're fighting a good fight for truth."

When his father told him he was "sticking his neck out very far" by joining the America Firsters, Gerstacker wrote back that he was quite aware of this "but someone has to do something to at least retard the horrible mistake we're

making." He was "in a difficult position," he admitted, "when it comes to discussing these things because I am in the Army, but come what may, as Carl Gerstacker, I shall fight this thing as long as I can."[5]

A quarter of a century later he would be one of the nation's leading internationalists, but as a young army officer he held quite the opposite view, violently opposed to the United States entering into what he perceived as a strictly European conflict.

He worked long hours at the Detroit office, and within a few months was able to report that "the Artillery Division is still a mess but it's getting better. The day just isn't long enough to get all the work done," he added. "Sometimes I think I'll just slide along like some other people do, but I just can't seem to do it."

Sometimes, he wrote his parents, it seemed to him that he was "in a dream from which I shall soon awake to find that life is normal again." As an example of the bewildering things that were happening to him, he said, "I spent this morning talking to [Harry] Coyle, the general manager of Chevrolet, Charley Wetherall, Chevrolet production superintendent, and Llewellyn, assistant to the man in charge of all General Motors War Production. I, Carl Gerstacker, was giving them pointers on how to produce equipment, and even got a little impatient (to myself, of course) because Mr. Coyle insisted on telling me all about Chevrolet and what they were doing. If I were working for General Motors, I probably wouldn't be important enough to tie Mr. Coyle's shoelaces. It's absolutely insane . . . tomorrow I'm going to Flint to tell the superintendent of Chevrolet there how to make guns, then to Buick to tell them how, then to Fisher Body in Grand Rapids, and finally to Duplex in Battle Creek. Am I really dreaming?"[6]

Inevitably his work and accomplishments were bringing him to the attention of the higher-ups in the Ordnance

Department. In the spring of 1942, he came into the office one morning to find a neatly typed memo on his desk signed by a half-dozen of his close associates. "Congratulations," it said, "CAPTAIN Gerstacker. May 21, 1942."[7]

A fortnight later he was summoned to Washington. General Campbell, the new chief of ordnance, felt that industrial concerns making the same or similar products should work together closely in wartime, freely exchanging information and helping each other in any way they could to increase their output and the quality of their products. If there were supply problems, for example, they should work together and arrange to move critical supplies where they were most needed. Under his plan the companies were to meet together and elect their own representatives, and the Ordnance Department would appoint an officer to work with each group.

Gerstacker was appointed to work with the manufacturers of 37 mm., 57 mm., 75 mm., and 3-inch mobile artillery carriages, most of which were located in the eastern half of the nation, all the way from Milwaukee, Wisconsin, to Tulsa, Oklahoma, to Biddeford-Saco, Maine. These manufacturing groups elected from among their membership a chairman who was located in Reading, Pennsylvania, so Gerstacker was promptly detached from Detroit and stationed in Reading to work with the manufacturers.[8] "In peacetime such activities would have been a flagrant violation of the antitrust laws," he said later, chuckling, "but this was wartime, and no one protested in the least."

From then on he was constantly on the move, from one artillery plant to the next, all across the eastern industrial belt where "his" plants were situated, always in the middle of any production problem that arose, serving as a full-time troubleshooter for the Ordnance Department. He loved it, and he was learning more about how to run a business than he could have learned in a decade or two in peacetime,

especially if he had been confined to one firm. Here he was encountering different people, different firms, different problems, day after day.

"I feel that every gun I get out may mean the difference between victory and defeat," he wrote home on one occasion. "It's like playing a game that I have to win. Only by trying harder than the other fellows can we be worthy of winning. Everything pales into significance beside the job of winning the war. . . . There's a principle that I like to follow in everything—always try harder than your opponent. If you're as adept as he, then you're sure to win, and if you're not as adept, you may win if you try harder."[9]

He served in this capacity for more than a year, until June 1943, when he was called to Washington once again. "No one explained to me before I went, the reason for my going," he wrote his parents.

It seems that the production section of the Carriage section of the Artillery branch was in trouble. The key men in it are a Major in charge, and a Captain and a high-priced civilian as assistants. The civilian was temporarily on a special job, the Captain wasn't working out so well, and the Major was a nervous wreck, so on the civilian's advice, the Colonel sent for Gerstacker. At first I considered a plan of just marking time so they wouldn't want me back, and then I felt so sorry for the Major that I pitched in and gave it my all. He was so pleased that they want me there all the time now. It's a little balled up because they've been ordered to get all officers of my youthful age [he was 26] out of Washington. They want me to be nominally in Reading but to spend most of my time in Washington. . . it makes me a little angry too because they keep complimenting me but don't promote me. Washington is a nut house. People rushing madly here and there without planning where or why they're going (I mean mentally as well as physically). . . .[10]

39

Life in crowded, frantic wartime Washington was especially difficult for a newcomer, but he rapidly adjusted to life in the "nut house" and to his new job. He was able to get a room there only "after a friend pulled some strings," and he had about a four-block walk to a bus which delivered him each day to the Pentagon, the then brand-new U.S. national defense headquarters. He ate all three meals a day at the Pentagon "because eating in Washington is not good." He went to a show by Bob Hope in Washington's Constitution Hall, he noted, "celebrating Ordnance Dept's 131st birthday," and he occasionally had dinner with Ruth Hale and her husband, Wiley Buchanan (later President Eisenhower's chief of protocol). Ruth was a friend from Midland and Herbert Dow's granddaughter. "They have nine cocker spaniels, six puppies, and a daughter Bonnie," he recorded.

The news from home was alarming. His father, who had been having "sick spells" brought on by heart disease for some years, suffered a heart attack in the summer of 1943 and after considerable anguish took his doctor's advice and retired. He was fifty-eight years old. "When I first read your letter, Dad, I was unhappy," Carl wrote his father from Washington, "but now I'm rather glad. You've talked of retiring and we've wanted you to retire for years. I'm afraid you would never have stopped unless something like this happened. You've always wanted and worked hard toward the goal of accumulating enough wherewithal to retire, and now you have plenty."

He advised his father by all means not to tell his boss "to go to hell"—his father had never liked or gotten along with the man who was his longtime boss at the Bartlett & Snow engineering firm, and had told his family many times that he would tell the man off "good and proper" when he retired. "Now that the time has come" his son advised, "the desire will not be as strong and you will part as friends."[11]

40

Ever since Pearl Harbor Day Carl had experienced strong "feelings of guilt," as great numbers of his friends and acquaintances were drafted and trained and sent overseas. "I feel like I'm making a contribution with what I'm doing, but how could I be so lucky as to spend the whole war in the U.S.," he wrote his parents, "while everyone else gets sent overseas?" He volunteered for overseas duty more than once, and in the fall of 1943 was actually sent to Aberdeen Proving Ground, Maryland, for what was called "field training"—basically training to live "in the field." For the first time in his military career he was given instruction in such basic military skills as firing a rifle. Nevertheless, he wrote home, "Am afraid my chances of going overseas are not very good. They have a lot of officers doing nothing but waiting for an assignment and many more who could be more easily replaced than I, and who are better trained for field duty."[12]

As it turned out, his superior officers in Washington refused to approve his assignment to overseas duty, and he stayed in his position there and in Reading. He kept asking why he had been doing a major's assignment for some months but was still a captain, and finally, in December of 1943, he wrote his parents, "My agitating seems to have stirred things up some, anyway. The Colonel and some of his henchmen advised me that he has put through a formal written request for my promotion. Is afraid they'll have trouble, though, because of my youth and the fact that promotions are supposed to be frozen. I have a suspicion that instead of Italy [where he had thought he might be sent after his field training], I'm apt to end up in Washington—what a miscarriage that would be."[13]

41

INTRODUCTION TO NEW YORK

Instead of Washington, he was assigned to the New York City office of the Ordnance Department, where he was to spend most of the rest of the war years riding herd on the department's suppliers, and there were many, in the Manhattan area. It was his first real exposure to New York and he hated it at first—it was hot and muggy and his sinuses were acting up—but he quickly fell in love with the place.

Within a few months he was reporting on a hectic round of activities. "Monday, I played bridge with some sharks at the Lexington Hotel," he wrote his parents. "Tuesday, I ate at the Auer's [Joe Auer was a married colleague] and played pinochle. Wednesday, we took two generals and a colonel to dinner. This afternoon, we toured New York harbor and the Army Port of Embarkation, and tonight I'm Officer of the Day."[14]

42

It was not long before he knew the New York area better than most of the natives, and thirty or forty years later he still knew where to go for a good breakfast at 5 A.M. (which was useful if you were appearing on the *Today Show*), and where to go if you were looking for odd-sized coffee filters or Italian diving gear.

He was at the big R. Hoe Company plant, up in the Bronx, when a hurricane struck in September 1944. "Boy, what a storm," he wrote home.

It's about 9:00 P.M. and a hurricane has been blowing up since 4:00 P.M. It's due to hit its top in about half an hour. I'm at the plant. We have sandbags around the doors and are expecting a flood at high tide, which is soon. The plant is right on the East River (at E. 138th St.) and it's rising fast. Furthermore, I'm supposed to take a sleeper to Boston at 12:30 A.M. Gosh I love a storm like this—back to the hatches, I'll write more later.

Friday morning. Well, the storm is over. We tramped all around the plant and watched the river until 10:00 P.M. last night and then I drove Joe (Auer) home. It was some drive!

Cars were stalled all along the way and once little Eda got down to a putt-putt but managed to keep going. Limbs and whole trees were over the roads. I was to meet two other fellows at Grand Central to leave for Boston and I had all the tickets. Got to the Pelham station at 11:00 P.M. to take the 11:08. When I asked about it they said there hadn't been a train since 6:00 P.M. I couldn't see driving down so I canceled the tickets and tried to page my friends. They wouldn't call them to the phone but they promised to try to tell them. After last night, I can really believe the hurricane stories. Of course most of the lights were out and you certainly get a thrill out of the wind screaming and the driving rain. Mother, you'd have loved it.[15]

He was still working hard for his oak leaves, gold oak leaves being the insignia of a major. When he was still wearing captain's bars in early 1945 he took the matter directly to General Campbell. "He was very nice, said he would make me Major tomorrow if he had vacancies," he wrote home. "He said my efficiency report was the highest he had ever seen."[16]

In the meantime, grief had come to his beloved "Unkie" and "Aunty" in Midland. Uncle Jim Pardee had been suffering from cancer for several years now, his body so bloated in the final months that he could barely walk. He died on 3 January 1944, leaving Aunt Elsa alone in their big new house on Midland's Main Street. But Aunty was also suffering from cancer, and succumbed to it on 2 October.

Uncle Jim left the bulk of his considerable fortune to his nearest relatives and to his favorite niece and nephew.

Elsa Pardee, by the terms of her will, set aside $1 million in Dow Chemical stock to establish the Elsa U. Pardee Foundation, which was to be devoted to "promotion of the control

43

and cure of cancer." Her nephew Carl became its treasurer, and served in that position for fifty-one years until his own death from a form of cancer. During the succeeding years much of his spare time was taken up with correspondence on these matters, principally with Gilbert A. Currie, the Midland attorney and friend who was the executor of their wills.

A few months later, as the war was winding down, Carl's father followed them, victim of another heart attack that this time carried him away. He was sixty years old. During his brief years of retirement he had followed the stock market avidly, picking out winners and losers as he and Carl had done a dozen years before, and writing his son with his recommendations so that they could compare notes as they had then.

"Dad, I'd like to see you set a new record for not having any of your spells," the son would write back. "I wish I knew the answer to your investment problem. What did you mean when you called Packard your 'albatross'? Why put any in Postal Savings? I thought it was messy to handle—wouldn't E Bonds or 2% savings be simpler? I think Standard of New Jersey, General Electric, & Industrial Rayon are good—not so happy about Sterling Drug. Wonder whether nylon and other plastics won't hurt rayon in long run—should be O.K. for awhile. A.T.&T. and Standard of Indiana should be safe enough. . . ."[17]

He had lost his closest friend and best adviser, his father, and he was not yet thirty.

Although the war was over, he did not feel like celebrating it. As it happened, on the day the war ended in Europe he was confined in the Bronx Area Station Hospital with what doctors diagnosed as "a mild form of pneumonia." On 9 May he wrote his mother that "the X-rays show that my chest is OK again and I'm ambulatory now, which means I can walk around. They said I would be out in a couple of days." He told her he had not seen a Protestant minister yet, "but a Jewish

rabbi comes in every day and is very nice and thoughtful—even gave me Protestant literature. A Catholic priest came in one day but left immediately as soon as he saw I wasn't Catholic. I have a feeling that they are pretty representative."[18]

As soon as he was able, he made arrangements for his mother to visit New York and was busily planning for all the sights he was going to show her. It was a trip they had talked about many times in the family—"when the war is over," they had always said, "and Dad is feeling up to it, you can show us New York"—except that Dad had always been included in the plans.

On 6 July, before his mother arrived for this bittersweet visit, he attended the New York wedding of Helen Dow which, he reported, "was very elegant. The groom, Macauley Whiting, is an Ensign, was captain of Yale football team this year, is from Birmingham, Mich. Reception at Waldorf included dancing and full dinner (that was a surprise). Many Midland people were there—Bennetts, Campbells, Brittons, Diehls, Heaths, Doans, Alden Dows, Kendalls, Looses, etc. Mrs. H. H. Dow couldn't make the trip. A number asked about you. The event took place here because of Navy troubles with the groom and the fact that Herby Dow (Herbert H. Dow II) is now at Yale. I took the Looses [William S. Loose, longtime magnesium sales manager for Dow] to dinner at New York Athletic Club Saturday. Played golf Thursday, Saturday, and today. Leave for Cincinnati tomorrow."[19]

45

The war in Europe was over, and the production of artillery slowed and then stopped as the war in the Pacific also came to its climax with the unleashing of the atomic bomb at Hiroshima.

But the army had one more task for Major Gerstacker. The Ordnance Department had reached the conclusion that all the big guns it had made should be stored away somewhere in case a war broke out again somewhere, sometime,

and they were needed. The well-respected A. D. Little Company, a research firm in Boston, was assigned the task of drawing up the plans for this storage program, and Gerstacker was assigned to A. D. Little "to teach them about artillery," as he put it. He did not think very highly of the project. "Of all the stupid things," he said many years later, "anybody who would think that the artillery of that day would fit the manner of war fifty years later, but we did it—we laid out a plan."

Looking back on it later, he said: "I had a wonderful experience in the Army . . . I spent all my time working with the companies and their executives trying to accomplish production and quality goals. It was a great education! It gave me a lot of self-confidence that I could do things where nobody knew me. Plus, in Midland, everybody knew how old I was, even though I had lost my hair early on. When I got in the Army, they thought I was a lot older than I was because I didn't have any hair. I had a chance to have more responsibility because I looked older."

46

His career in the military service was such a great success that he more than once seriously considered staying in the army when the war was over. "I would have needed only about 12 more years until I would get a pension; I could have retired after 20 years of service. I didn't figure we'd have another war in the next 12 years, so it would be kind of a nice life. I would go to college, take courses, and fool around. I seriously thought of that and debated it."

While he was considering these matters he received a letter from Steve Starks, the head Dow personnel recruiter for many years, saying that Dow "would like to hire me back. There was a rule that companies had to hire their servicemen back. I thought that I did like it at Dow, so maybe I ought to go back there to work."[20]

On 1 May 1946 he was finally discharged from the U.S. Army. He headed directly for Midland and Dow.

4

The Mentor,
1946–59

1946   On 26 August transfers to Dow's Purchasing Department as expeditor. Resumes efforts to move to financial sector.

1947   Willard Dow, company CEO, sends him to Texas Division of company with mission of revising its reports to Midland so that they are "understandable." Although he has never been to Texas before, successfully accomplishes this mission and begins a rapid ascent of the company ladder.

1948   Willard Dow, complaining that Earl W. Bennett, Dow treasurer and the company's financial genius, "won't tell me what's going on in the financial part of this company," forms a Finance Committee with Bennett as chairman and appoints Gerstacker as a member. This inaugurates a mentor relationship for Gerstacker that lasts the rest of Bennett's long life. On 15 June is elected to Dow's board of directors. Is elected as 1949 president of Midland Rotary Club, as 1949 president of Midland chapter of American Red Cross, and as 1949 president of Dow Chemical Employees' Credit Union.

1949   In February is appointed assistant treasurer of company. Shortly afterward, on 31 March, Willard Dow is killed when his plane crashes in bad weather near London, Ontario, and a major reorganization of the company occurs, with Leland I. Doan becoming the new president and CEO. Bennett, who had been contemplating retirement as treasurer at age sixty-nine, instead becomes chairman of the board and Gerstacker succeeds him as company treasurer at age thirty-two.

1950   On 22 October marries Jayne Harris Cunningham. Wedding takes place in Omaha, Nebraska, at home of bride's married sister. Serving as best man is his brother-in-law, Bill Allen, for whom he had been best man in 1936.

1951   When a Japanese delegation arrives in Midland to propose a joint venture to manufacture saran in Japan, Gerstacker opposes it violently, the memory of the war still vivid. L. I. Doan promptly names Gerstacker chairman of the Dow

negotiating team. Asahi-Dow Ltd. is incorporated in early 1952 as Dow's first joint venture abroad. On 18 August Jayne delivers their first child, Bette Mignon Gerstacker.

1952   On 9 September is elected a director and treasurer of the Saran Yarns Company, Odenton, Maryland, a joint venture of Dow and National Plastic Products Company, the first of multitudinous appointments as an officer of Dow-associated firms and subsidiaries.

1955   On 25 August is elected a vice president of Dow. On 29 November a second daughter arrives and is named Lisa Jayne Gerstacker.

Inaugurates the Gerstacker teacher awards, given annually to outstanding teachers in the Midland public school system.

1957   On 8 March his sister Elsa dies suddenly of heart failure at age forty-five. In May is named to the Executive Committee, the "inner circle" of the Dow company's management. In June receives an honorary doctorate from Central Michigan University in Mt. Pleasant. (It is the first of six honorary doctorates he will receive, the others being conferred by Albion College, Northwood University, University of Michigan, Waynesburg [Pennsylvania] College, and Alma College.) At Christmas holiday he and his mother establish the Rollin M. Gerstacker Foundation with other family members as their fellow trustees, and authorize its first grants, totaling $875.

49

1959   At the first of the year, purchases the L. I. Doan house at 1018 W. Main Street and moves his family there. Makes a gift of the Pardee house, where they have been living, to Memorial Presbyterian Church and it becomes the Presbyterian manse. On 18 April, with mother, funds a cottage for boys at the Starr Commonwealth for Boys in memory of Elsa. On 17 December succeeds Bennett as chairman of the Dow Finance Committee.

T HE DOW CHEMICAL COMPANY THAT GERSTACKER CAME
back to in the summer of 1946, after his military service, was in a state of considerable confusion. Now that
the war was over, men who had worked for the firm were
flooding back from the military services, and there was little
or no advance warning of who or how many might arrive on
a given day. As a result, there was little or no opportunity to
prepare for their arrival. In addition, the company was losing
its wartime customers right and left (more than ninety percent of its wartime output had gone to the military services),
and it was readjusting to peacetime living as rapidly as it
could.

"To my horror, they had far more people than they knew
what to do with," Gerstacker said. "They didn't even need
what they had, let alone hiring servicemen back. When I
came, they didn't need me. I was like a hole in their head. I
came back to work and for a few days I just sat there."

Then one day, he said,

the unbelievable happened to me. Willard Dow, who was the
CEO and in charge of everything, called me to his office and
said, "Come on with me." He walked up a flight of stairs to the
Purchasing Department and called on the head of that department (Milton E. [Milt] LeFevre). Willard was the head of the
company, but he sat down across from the head of the
Purchasing Department and started telling him what a wonderful person I was. He said I had a great war record and all that
sort of thing, and how the Purchasing Department really
needed somebody like me. The whole time, the purchasing
head's expression got worse and worse, as I watched. I was being
sold like somebody on the block by the head of the company!
I thought this was a strange thing that I was going through,
because I had dealt with a lot of company heads and executives
during the war.

After awhile, Willard Dow could also see that the head of the Purchasing Department was not very interested, so, all of a sudden, he jumped to his feet and said, "Come on, we want to go down the hall," and we left. I thought, "This is a strange company." We walked down the hall and went to the Production Engineering Department. Again we sat across from the head of the department (Wilfred M. [Fred] Murch) and Willard Dow went through the same selling talk, trying to talk this guy into accepting me. This guy did not have as much guts as the head of the Purchasing Department, so he took me. But he didn't know what to do with me.

My job was to get out more production. I had a certain number of plants I would call on. Their biggest trouble was not that they couldn't make the stuff, but that they couldn't get the required shipping containers, which were paper containers shaped like drums. I thought that situation was ridiculous, so I went down to the same head of the Purchasing Department and told him what a no-good he was at getting those containers. I enjoyed doing that! After I had done that a couple of times, he got mad and said, "If you think you're so smart, I'll give you a job in this department. You go get those containers. Nobody else can do it. Let's see how good you are." I said, "Fine," and I went to work for him. I called on the company that made the containers and got some. For awhile I was doing that kind of job in the Purchasing Department.[1]

51

While working in the Purchasing Department he resumed his efforts to move to the financial side. "I just used every opportunity and relationship that came up to get involved with the financial part of the company," he said. "I very much followed it up and tried very hard."

His big break came a few months later. Willard Dow, continuing his unorthodox methods, called Gerstacker to his office and said, "Look at these reports! I'm getting these from

[Albert P. (Dutch)] Beutel, who runs the Texas Division. He is telling me what his capacity is and that he wants to build more plants, but I can't understand these reports. I don't think you could either. Take them and see. I think we've got to do something to straighten out that situation, so I want you to go to Texas and straighten Beutel out. See that he writes reports from now on that I can understand."

Gerstacker said later, "I almost died! Here I was, a young person with a not very big job in the Purchasing Department, and Dutch Beutel was a great hero. He ran the huge Texas Division and everybody was afraid of him, and here was Willard Dow telling me I should go to Texas and straighten him out. I had never even been to Texas. I couldn't believe he was serious, but he was, so I went to Texas."

In Texas he reported to Beutel and told him he had come from Willard Dow with orders to revise the reports that he sent to Midland. "I thought he was going to hit me," Gerstacker said. Beutel finally assigned some of his key men to work with him and they went to work.

"It was a hot, humid, horrible summer," Gerstacker said.

I asked, "What is your plant capacity?" They answered, "It depends if you look at it this way, or if you look at it that way." We were working all day long, but when I got through I didn't know anything. Nobody told me anything! It dawned on me after a while that Beutel had probably said, "Don't tell this guy from Midland anything." I wasn't learning anything or getting anywhere. After a few days, with a straight face, I announced that we really weren't making the kind of progress that I had expected, and I thought we ought to start working nights in addition to days. They went back to Beutel, obviously, and reported that the plan wasn't working, that the guy wasn't going to go home, and that he wasn't getting discouraged. Then they redesigned all the reports. I didn't do it; they did it. I came back

to Midland and showed the reports to Willard Dow, who thought they were wonderful. He now understood them and he thought I had done a great job. But I hadn't done anything. They had done it all in Texas.

Shortly after this, Willard Dow called him in again, and he said, "Mr. [Earl W.] Bennett is a wonderful man and he is very smart, but he leads me around like there is a ring in my nose. He makes me do things I don't want to do. He won't tell me what's happening in the financial part of this company. I don't think that's right. If we have an issue coming up, he takes the side that he doesn't believe in because he knows I will disagree with him. Then when I disagree with him, he finally gives in to me, but that's what he wanted in the first place. It makes me so mad!" Once again Gerstacker thought to himself, "This is a wild company that I'm working for." Willard Dow said, "I'm going to start a Finance Committee, so other people can find out what's going on with the finances of this company, and I'm going to put you on that Finance Committee."

53

The company had not had a Finance Committee prior to this time. In reality, Earl Bennett had made all the financial decisions. Bennett became the chairman of the Finance Committee, along with Charlie Penhaligen, Fred H. Brown, the head accountant, H. S. (Doc) Kendall, Willard's chief administrative aide, Gerstacker, and Calvin A. (Tink) Campbell, head of the Legal Department.[2]

"All of us were supposed to be a Finance Committee, but nobody told us what we were supposed to do, except Willard Dow, who said, 'Find out what's happening in the company.' When we had our first meeting with Mr. Bennett, he didn't know what we should discuss. He didn't even want a Finance Committee. We had a terrible time for a while, but finally that worked out and we had a Finance Committee that did things.

Willard Dow began to get reports and he guessed that maybe some of us were learning something about the finances of the company."

COMPANY TREASURER

By February of 1949 both Earl Bennett and Willard Dow felt comfortable enough with Gerstacker that they quietly conferred on him the title of assistant treasurer of the Dow company. He had already become a member of the company's board of directors a year earlier, in June 1948, when the size of the board was expanded from nine directors to fourteen to reflect the mushrooming growth of the company—sales had climbed from $25 million in 1938, when he joined the company, to $170 million in 1948, only ten years later.[3]

A few weeks later the company was turned upside down when an airplane crash wiped out its leader. Willard Dow was a member of the Corporation of Massachusetts Institute of Technology and attended its meetings in Boston regularly. In addition his son, Herbert H. Dow II, was a student at the school, so he flew there frequently. On 31 March, despite a bad weather report, a Dow company plane took off from Midland on a foggy winter's morning and winged its way toward Boston. Winston Churchill was visiting MIT that day, and Willard Dow had been informed that he would be seated beside the great man at lunch, an event that Willard was looking forward to with keen anticipation. It is indeed most unlikely that he would have insisted on flying to Boston that day except for this circumstance. Over London, Ontario, the wings of the plane were icing up badly and the pilot tried desperately to land at the airport there but crashed in the fog. Willard and his wife Martha were killed instantly, as were the pilot and co-pilot, Fred C. (Blackie) Clements and Arthur

54

J. Bowie, and Mrs. Calvin A. Campbell. Tink Campbell was the only survivor

Among those totally devastated by the loss was the remaining leadership of the Dow company. Willard Dow had been its uncontested chief since the death of his father in 1930 and now was suddenly snuffed out in the prime of his powers.

After the funeral a sorrowful Dow board of directors gathered to pick up the pieces. Leland I. (Lee) Doan, Willard's brother-in-law, who had been the company's sales manager for twenty years, became the new president and chief executive. "There has to be a lot of sharing of this burden," Doan told the board. Mark E. Putnam, the production chief, moved up to general manager. Tink Campbell, general counsel, became corporate secretary, replacing Doan.

Earl Bennett, who was then sixty-nine and thinking about retiring, instead found himself promoted to chairman of the board, the crowning achievement of a fabulous career. He had begun as an office boy a half-century before. The directors promoted their newly appointed assistant treasurer, Carl Gerstacker, to replace Bennett as treasurer. Bennett would remain as chairman of the Financial Committee. "The company didn't want to look outside for a treasurer, and I was all they had," Gerstacker said later.

"We were all dispirited," Gerstacker said years later, "It was a time of extreme gravity for our company; in fact, some people wondered whether Dow Chemical would survive this crisis. Lee Doan picked us up off the floor and led our company to unprecedented heights of achievement and prosperity."[4]

55

THE LOVE BUG BITES

His mother had been asking him for years when he was going to get married. "You seem to go out with all sorts of girls," she

wrote him in 1942, when he was a dashing, twenty-six-year-old army captain "What kind of girl are you looking for?" He thought about it and wrote back, "Sometimes I think that my standards are too high. I want the girl to be a very graceful dancer, have an intelligent and alert mind, a college education, a nice family, carry herself and dress well, be clean, and enjoy the kind of friends that I do. There are probably a few (things) I've left out too. I think it's all patterned after you, Mother."[5]

By 1950 he was thirty-four years old and the rising young star of the Dow Chemical Company, beginning now to settle into bachelorhood, but still dating "all sorts of girls," night after night, and Mother was still asking, "What kind of girl are you looking for?" She was sixty-five years old, and her only son wasn't married yet.

When he joyfully announced to her that he was in love and had finally found the girl he was going to marry, Mother found it hard to believe, but recovered soon enough and plunged enthusiastically into the wedding plans, as mothers will.

The girl who met the requirements he had stipulated years before was Jayne Harris Cunningham, wife of William C. Cunningham, a design engineer at the Dow Corning Corporation in Midland. Their marriage had not lasted long and they were in the midst of a divorce proceeding. The story told in the family was that Carl was dating another of those fetching Harris sisters, Edith, and one evening he and "Edie" went out dancing with Edie's sister, Jayne, and her soon-to-be-divorced husband, Bill. Jayne and Carl were smitten with each other immediately, and when the evening was over Carl escorted home a delighted Jayne, leaving Edie and Bill to their own devices.

The Harris girls were the daughters of Mr. and Mrs. Walter Lowrie Harris of Omaha, Nebraska, and the bride and groom

56

decided to go to Omaha for the wedding, to be followed by a honeymoon in Hawaii. The wedding was set for 22 October 1950, at the home of Mr. and Mrs. Howard Drew, another of Jayne's sisters, in Omaha. Bill Allen served as best man, returning the favor Carl had done him at his sister Elsa's wedding fourteen years before. The Reverend Harold T. Janes of Omaha's First Central Congregational Church presided.

The wedding was followed by a buffet supper. Then the wedding party left to attend Nebraska's biggest gala of the season, the Aksarben Coronation Ball. Eda and Elsa, his mother and sister, hosted a family dinner the night before the wedding. Three days later the newlyweds sailed on the *Lurline* from San Francisco for Hawaii. Three weeks later they returned to the Pardee house on Midland's Main Street, which was to be their home, and he went back to work.[6]

THE MENTOR   57

With the formation of the Finance Committee in 1948, followed by Gerstacker's rapid promotions to assistant treasurer and treasurer of the firm, he found himself working ever more frequently and closely with Earl Bennett, the living legend who was held literally in awe by the financial and accounting departments of the company.

Bennett, a tiny man barely five feet tall, had been born in a lumber camp at White Cloud, Michigan, in 1880. His father drove horses for the camp and his mother helped the camp cook. He began working in the camps at age sixteen and never finished high school, working as camp cook because he was too small to be a lumberjack, and saving every penny he could. When he had accumulated $450 he left the lumberjack trade and went to Chicago, where he enrolled in a two-year accounting course at the Bryant Stratton Business

College. He finished the course in one year and was working at Marshall Field's in Chicago for $500 a year when he visited his grandmother in the Midland area and discovered there the small but rapidly growing Dow Chemical Company, in 1900 only three years old. Herbert Dow offered him a job as office boy at $360 a year, but Bennett took it in spite of the salary cut because, as he said, he had a feeling that he would like to "grow up with this company."

By 1 January 1901 he was the company bookkeeper, a year later its auditor, by 1907 assistant secretary and assistant treasurer of the firm, and from then until 1959 its financial brain.

"Bennett was an amazing financial genius," Gerstacker said. "As H. H. Dow's office boy he started keeping the books on the side. The books were originally kept in Cleveland because the Cleveland people didn't trust H. H. Dow. But H. H. and Bennett began keeping another set of books in Midland. There were then two sets of books, but the two didn't agree. Finally Bennett and the Cleveland people got together. They found Bennett was better than they were, so they let him keep the books in Midland. That man was an absolute genius and we learned so much from him."[7]

"He was a little tyrant in a way, which fooled a lot of people," Gerstacker said.

> He had mostly "yes men" around him. He didn't want "yes men" but he tested people to find out if they would fight with him. If they didn't, then he lost a lot of respect for them. He didn't have many strong people around him. He liked to start with the answers and work back. I used to be tremendously amused. He would say to me, "Carl, I think we ought to do such-and-so," and he would give me some reasons for doing it. I used to look at the reasons and see that they didn't make sense. They were absolutely wrong! I would discover some mistakes, but he would not pay any attention when I tried to point them out. It finally

dawned on me that he had only filled in some things to fit the conclusion he had started with. It didn't matter what the facts were, he knew the right answer. That was the way he did things.

When a security analyst would come in to ask Bennett about the company, he would let Gerstacker sit in on the meeting "so that I could learn," Gerstacker said. "The guy would ask a question like, 'Epsom salts are doing poorly, aren't they, so is that a bad product?' Bennett would sit there and nod and start to answer the question, but he would never get to the question. Instead he would talk about the latest invention until the outsider's eyes would get really interested in what Bennett was saying. Pretty soon the security analyst had forgotten his question and he would never get back to it. He would be off talking about this other new thing. It was just marvelous! Bennett was something!"

Gerstacker frequently argued with Bennett, which the old man loved. "I guess I was the most aggressive one on the financial committee," Gerstacker said. "I pushed harder, so he began to adopt me, after a while, and accept me."

The early 1950s were a period of intensive learning for him, not only in his apprenticeship to Bennett but in many other ways, and he began to develop as well an ability to reverse his field quite drastically in a relatively short period of time.

Perhaps the most dramatic example of this education occurred in the fall of 1951, when a delegation from Japan came to Midland to propose that Dow and the Japanese join in building a plant in Japan to produce saran. The Japanese said they had a tremendous need for saran in this postwar period for the manufacture of fishing nets, a critical element in a key Japanese industry, to produce a key element in the Japanese diet. Many Dow executives were openly dubious of the proposal. The use of saran to make fishnets was a concept

59

they had never heard before, and it did not help that the Japanese delegation was led by Manabu Enseki, who had been first minister of Japan in the United States at the time of Pearl Harbor and was listed as "persona non grata" by the U.S. government. He had figured in a famous photograph on the steps of the U.S. Capitol featuring Japanese diplomats who were holding discussions with the U.S. government in Washington at the time Japanese planes were already on their way to attack Pearl Harbor. The delegation had waited in Canada for several months while the Japanese attempted to obtain permission for Enseki to enter the United States.

Gerstacker was furious. Only five years before he had been an officer in the army that was fighting Tojo and his friends, he said, and he felt that any business firm that joined hands with them now would be seen as being willing to do anything, even to the extent of collaborating with its worst enemies, to further its affairs. When the matter was brought before the Dow board of directors for a decision, he led the opposition and lost. Following a spirited discussion, the board voted to enter into negotiations with the Japanese toward the formation of a jointly owned firm to manufacture saran in Japan.

Gerstacker was stunned, therefore, when Lee Doan appointed him chairman of the Dow Negotiating Committee, but he accepted in good grace, and the negotiations got under way. Still not ready to accept defeat, he decided the best way he could scuttle the whole business was to lay down terms that were so patently advantageous to Dow and disadvantageous to the Japanese that the Japanese could not possibly accept them, and he opened the negotiations with a speech laying down such terms.

To his surprise the Japanese talked excitedly to each other at great length, in Japanese, and perspired greatly, and then announced that they were accepting his terms. Early in 1952 Asahi-Dow Ltd. was incorporated. It was the first joint venture

60

for Dow outside the North American continent and one of the earliest, if not the earliest, such venture in postwar Japan. It also proved to be one of the most successful.

It was also, for Gerstacker, the beginning of a long and fruitful relationship with the Japanese that was to culminate in his receiving the Order of the Rising Sun from Emperor Hirohito some twenty-five years later. Over time he reversed his opinion of the Japanese, and he also reversed his opinions about debt. "My parents and grandparents drilled into me as deeply as anything the principle that I should never be in debt," he said.

> You didn't buy anything until you had saved up the money so you could pay cash. It might be necessary to have a mortgage on your home but if so, you hurried to pay it off and were just a little ashamed to walk down the street until you owned your home free and clear. When I visited my German relatives in Bavaria I quickly found out that debt to them was almost the worst sin. They whispered about a neighbor who was in debt as if he lacked morality.
>
> So, with the firm belief that I should never be in debt in any fashion, I got a job at Dow Chemical. I loved my work but I felt guilty from the debt standpoint because I had relatives and many friends working at the company and I was afraid that they were helping me. After a couple of years I had about decided to quit because of this and go to work for some other company. Fortunately for me the army hired me for about six years and this experience resolved some of my debt feelings so that I was more or less at peace coming back to Dow to work. During my army days I was known as a very square person because I would never allow anyone to buy me a lunch unless I bought him one in return and I would never accept any gifts.
>
> Then I went to work for Earl Bennett. He taught me that owing money was sound and smart and that there was nothing

61

morally wrong with it. I finally rationalized my ethics into believing that debt was okay as far as money was concerned but I continued to believe that favors or gifts must be avoided or immediately compensated for to keep the slate even.[8]

Bennett believed that "the more money you could borrow, the better. He thought you should always be in debt, because then you used other people's capital and you paid them interest. He convinced me he was right and that all my past education had been wrong."[9]

He also began to build a reputation as the Dow company's leading exponent of thrift. If it wasn't really needed the company should not buy it, he contended. For example, for many years after the airplane crash that killed Willard Dow, the company's board of directors refused to buy any more company planes. For a long time there was an unspoken rule on the subject, a conviction that whatever Dow might have learned from the loss of its leader, it was not about to plunge into the "company plane business" again very soon. To do so would be an affront to the memory of Willard Dow.

Dutch Beutel, general manager of the gigantic Texas Division of Dow, was perhaps most directly affected by the rule, and the most vocal about it. He had to make his way to Midland once a month for the meeting of the board of directors and then back again to Texas, and by train or commercial air flights it took a full day or two each way, and he estimated that he was spending at least ten percent of his time just traveling back and forth from Texas to Midland. "I want to be able to get up here to Midland before I've forgotten what I was mad about," Beutel complained. But each time he brought up the question he was silenced by the majority of his colleagues.

Eventually, however, Beutel managed to win over the majority of his colleagues—except for Gerstacker, the last

holdout. The board then authorized Beutel to buy a plane, the first the company had owned since Willard's death, and when it arrived in Midland he proudly invited Gerstacker to come and see it. Gerstacker groaned, but went to look anyway. Beutel had christened the plane the "CAG," and these letters were painted prominently on its nose. Gerstacker took one look at what Beutel had done and burst into laughter.

He was always willing to take defeat gracefully and to laugh with the rest when the joke was on him.

In the succeeding years Gerstacker gradually took over the financial reins from Bennett and steadily built his stature in the company.

GROWTH YEARS

A year after the Asahi-Dow episode the company entered into another joint venture, the Saran Yarns Company, established at Odenton, Maryland, in collaboration with the National Plastic Products Co. Gerstacker, who had once more been involved in the negotiations, became a director and treasurer of the firm. It was the first of a long series of such appointments for him as the Dow company invented and expanded and spun off new firms to make and market those inventions.

63

As the company looked for an entrée into the consumer business—its first consumer product, in the mid-1950s, was Saran Wrap—Gerstacker and Bill Dixon, then the rising star of the Dow Marketing Department, decided the best way to move into the consumer trade was to acquire an already established consumer business to build on. Gerstacker and Dixon looked at various possibilities and decided their best possibility was the French perfume and fashion house, Chanel.

Gerstacker thereupon began to court Pierre Wertheimer, a distinguished old French gentleman then in his seventies

who owned many French properties, including Chanel. Gerstacker went to Paris and met him, and they got along well, and he took him to dinner at Lutece in New York, and other fine places, during the courtship. Wertheimer had only one son, but considered him a dummy and was afraid he would inherit the business and promptly ruin it. The negotiations were going well and Gerstacker was about to get Dow into the perfume and fashion business (Coco Chanel came with the package), when the old man up and died.

Gerstacker met with the son and heir, who did not consider himself a dummy at all, and as it turned out had no inclination whatever to close the deal with Dow. The whole thing fell apart. Gerstacker was not too disappointed because he had some misgivings about the Dow company running a chemical business in one hand and dispensing Chanel No. 5 with the other, he said later. "But Chanel was so prestigious and so profitable that it would have been good for us," he added.

As it turned out, Gerstacker had earned his way into the Dow leadership just as the company was about to undergo one of its most significant periods of expansion, and he was about to become involved in a number of projects related to this growth.

1950 Dow acquires Bush Aromatics, Inc., of Jersey City, N.J.

1951 Dow contracts with the Atomic Energy Commission to build and operate a plant at Rocky Flats, Colorado, for the AEC.

1952 Dow plant at Allyn's Point, Connecticut, begins production of Styron polystyrene plastic for the eastern U.S. market. In addition, the company establishes Dow Chemical Inter-American and Dow Chemical International Ltd., at Midland, which will be the major vehicles for expansion of its businesses around the world,

and mark the beginning of the company's growth into a truly global firm.

1953 Dow plant at Torrance, California, inaugurates production of Styron for the western U.S. market. Dow opens the world's largest magnesium rolling mill and wrought products plant at Madison, Illinois, in a facility it purchases from the U.S. government.

1954 Dow purchases Versenes, Inc., at Framingham, Massachusetts—its introduction to the manufacture of chelating compounds.

1955 A big new plant for the production of Saran Wrap is opened in Midland as this product is launched nationally. Saran Wrap will become the flagship of the new Dow consumer products division, and Dow products begin showing up on supermarket shelves around the world. In Europe, the company establishes Nederlandse Dow Maatschappij N. V. at Rotterdam, the Netherlands. This company—NDM—will operate a port facility, the Botlek, for Dow products arriving from the United States and Canada for European markets. Once a healthy market for a product is established in Europe, Dow will build a plant or plants in Europe to manufacture it.

65

1956 A period of intensive plant construction begins at Dow installations around the world. Plants at Hanging Rock, Ohio, and Plaquemine, Louisiana, are under construction. A new company headquarters complex, which will eventually be dubbed the Dow Center, is built on a 160-acre site a few miles from the original headquarters in Midland. A plant to make Zefran fiber is going up near Lee Hall, Virginia. Bay Refining Company and its associated firm, Bay Pipe Line Corp., in Bay City, Michigan, are acquired by Dow as a source of petrochemical feedstocks for the Midland manufacturing area.

1957 Texas Division of Dow begins production of acetylene. Hanging Rock and Riverside, Missouri, plants open for Styrofoam production, doubling Dow's capacity for one of its most popular products, Styrofoam. Company begins building ethylene and linear polyethylene plants at Bay City, which will soon become the largest petro-chemical facility east of the Mississippi. The company initiates its matching-grants-to-education program. Dow acquires the Dobeckmun Company of Cleveland, which becomes the core of its packaging division. Company acquires a government-owned magnesium production plant at Velasco, Texas, for $20.7 million.

1958 Dow opens a new marine terminal at Bay City as Midland prepares to take advantage of the new St. Lawrence Seaway facilities to ship products around the world. In Canada, Dow forms Rio Tinto-Dow Ltd., a joint venture established by the Rio Tinto Mining Company of Canada, Ltd., and Dow Chemical of Canada, to produce thorium and rare earths from by-products of uranium mining in the Blind River area of Ontario.[10]

It seemed as though the growth of the company would never slow down, and it didn't for the next two decades. It was not until 1975 that Gerstacker saw any deceleration. "I think there is less push for us to expand now," he said in 1975. "I think our percentage growth outside the U.S. will slow from what it has been, but I think we will continue to grow faster outside the U.S. than in the U.S."[11]

In 1955 Gerstacker was elected a vice president of the company, and in 1957 he was appointed a member of the company's Executive Committee, the inner circle of the company's top management. He was forty years old.

His family was also growing at this time. Although Jayne proved to have severe problems during childbirth, she

delivered their first child, Bette Mignon Gerstacker, on 18
August 1951, and their second, Lisa Jayne Gerstacker, on 29
November 1955. She lost other babies, and one was stillborn.
He and Jayne were happy to have two healthy girls to raise, and
he added a couple of bedrooms and a bathroom on the Pardee
house to accommodate them. There was also a "secret" circular staircase so that the children could reach their rooms or
leave them without going through the main part of the house,
where meetings of one sort or another might be going on.

His sister Elsa, married to Bill Allen, had had severe kidney problems for many years, but it was a complete shock
when she had a heart attack in March 1957 and died a few
days later at the Henry Ford Hospital in Detroit, at the age of
forty-five. She was a graduate of Oberlin College in Ohio and
had done post-graduate work at Vassar. She had taught pre-
school in Midland until her marriage.

She had been a devoted trustee of the Pardee Foundation,
of which she was vice president, and until her death she did
most of the work of investigating the proposed recipients of
grants to carry on the cancer research sponsored by the foundation. After her death the foundation formed a committee
of cancer experts to review the proposals, a practice which
continues today.

Like her brother, Elsa was deeply involved in community
and church. She was the founding president of the Clytean
Club, one of the city's leading women's organizations, and
had been president of the Midland chapter of the American
Association of University Women and of the Little Garden
Club. She was a deacon in the Memorial Presbyterian Church.
In an editorial published after her death, the *Midland Daily
News* recounted her contributions to the community and said,
"Mrs. Allen will be missed by many, who will long remember
her as a sparkling personality who was with us much too short
a time. She was a cheerful and a friendly person who made

67

you glad that you knew her. She radiated to others that intangible something that might be called 'zest for living.'"[12]

A few months later, much to his surprise, an honorary doctor of laws degree was conferred on Gerstacker by Central Michigan College (now University) in Mt. Pleasant. It was to be the first of six honorary degrees he would receive during his lifetime, and "like anything you do," he said, "the first time is always a big thrill."

He stood solemnly as Dr. Charles L. Anspach, president of the institution, read the citation. "The greatness of a scientist and an engineer may be measured by his revelations of the intricate and hitherto unknown structural relations of the physical world and by his skill in mobilizing human intelligence to give utility to that new knowledge," Dr. Anspach said. "By the strictest standards, Carl Allan Gerstacker, vice president and treasurer of the Dow Chemical Company, attains greatness." Gerstacker's financial contributions, he noted, "have been exceedingly generous, but often, according to close friends, anonymously given. Among his fellow scientists and business associates, he is known and respected especially for his high intelligence, his forthrightness, his keen perception of the changing demands in chemical research and industry, his integrity, and his friendliness."[13]

The Christmas holidays seemed rather empty that year of 1957, with Elsa gone, but the family gathered as usual to celebrate, and the calendar as usual included the meeting of the Pardee Foundation, which by this time had become an integral part of their annual festivities. This time, he and his mother had a special announcement to make. Eda had decided she wanted to establish a new and separate foundation, not restricted to the fight against cancer, and she was naming it in honor of her late husband. It would therefore be known as the Rollin M. Gerstacker Foundation, and at least at the beginning would have the same officers as the Elsa

U. Pardee Foundation. It would be dedicated to carrying on, "indefinitely, financial aid to charities of all types supported by Mr. and Mrs. R. M. Gerstacker during their lifetimes."

In that first year the brand new Gerstacker Foundation made four grants totaling $875: $250 to the Starr Commonwealth for Boys at Albion, Michigan, $225 to the Midland Community Fund, $200 to the Midland Hospital, and $200 to the Memorial Presbyterian Church in Midland for its Maintenance Fund.[14]

Over the next forty-five years, keeping its funds invested heavily in Dow Chemical stock and benefiting greatly from major bequests by Eda Gerstacker and later from Carl, the foundation became one of the ten largest in the state of Michigan and distributed in that time more than $100 million in grants.

BLACK FRIDAY   69

A sudden and severe economic recession hit the United States in the late months of 1957, just as Dow's spending for expansion was reaching its peak. The company had been hiring new employees at a brisk pace, doubling its employee population from 13,500 in 1949 to 27,000 in 1957. As Dow sales began to fall off, the company was quite unexpectedly caught in a vise between a rapidly diminishing flow of income and the rising tide of expense for expansion and a growing payroll. It was the first time the company had encountered such a crisis, and it was clearly one that called for drastic action.

And it was drastic action that the Dow board took. It decided on the following measures: (1) to "stretch out," or slow down, as much of the construction program as it could without incurring heavy losses; (2) to order an immediate stop to all recruiting of new employees; and (3) for the first

time in company history mandated a general reduction in personnel, to total ten percent. The program was announced on Friday, 23 May 1958, remembered by employees for many years after as "Black Friday." Each department head, companywide, was to accomplish a ten percent reduction in his or her department by evaluating the performance of each employee in the department and dismissing those that fell to the bottom. The whole operation was to be completed within ninety days (and it was).

On the negative side, it was a traumatic experience for all the employees, and it ruined Dow's reputation on the nation's campuses. For many years the company had problems recovering its access to the best potential employees.

As a result of all this, understaffing became a way of life at Dow, and whether measured in sales or earnings per employee or other measurements, Dow employees invariably led the chemical industry in these measures in succeeding years. Gerstacker promised the employees that "another 1958" would not happen as long as he was around, and for the remainder of his career at Dow he made sure this was true. It was a promise that he repeated many times in the course of his talks to employee groups.

He and the younger members of the top management remembered it as a great learning experience. "What a lesson that was, when the bottom fell out of everything and Dow fired 10 percent of everybody across the board," Ted Doan said. "We had never fired anybody in our lives as a company, and this made all the universities mad at us. It was good in the sense that it gave a lot of people the determination never to let that happen again."[15]

By the fall of 1958 the economy had bounced back and Dow quickly resumed its rapid expansion and its hiring programs. But Gerstacker and many others never forgot Black Friday.

70

5

THE TROIKA, 1960–67

1960   Major shakeup in Dow leadership is precipitated by death of Mark E. Putnam, seventy-four, executive vice president of the firm, on 6 November, and decision by Bennett, who has reached the age of eighty, to retire. On 11 November Gerstacker is elected chairman of the board, succeeding Bennett. Herbert D. (Ted) Doan, thirty-eight, becomes executive vice president.

Three days later, on 14 November, Gerstacker begins a two-year term as president of Synthetic Organic Chemical Manufacturers Association (SOCMA).

On 29 December is appointed a director of the Detroit branch of the Federal Reserve Bank of Chicago for a three-year term.

1961   On 15 May resigns from Midland hospital board of directors after twelve years of service as director and treasurer.

On 21 June, with then-vice president Lyndon B. Johnson and Lady Bird, presides over dedication of plant to produce potable water from seawater at Freeport, Texas.

1962   On 12 September, at Dow's annual meeting of stockholders, L. I. Doan announces his retirement. Ted Doan is elected as new president and CEO and C. B. (Ben) Branch as executive vice president. Gerstacker remains as board chairman. This puts in place the "troika"—Doan, Branch, and Gerstacker—which manages the company jointly for the next sixteen years and more.

In April testifies before the House Ways and Means Committee against a bill slashing tariffs on chemical products.

1963   Rejoins board of directors of Chemical State Savings Bank, Midland, at end of service with Federal Reserve Bank.

Leads Dow into the banking business, signing contract with Bankierskantoor Mendes Gans, a private bank in Amsterdam of which Dow acquires forty percent. BMG becomes Dow's currency clearinghouse in Europe.

1964   Dow board of directors travels to Zurich for its November meeting, to get better acquainted with Europe and underline Dow's rapid growth as an international company.

1965   Dow company is reorganized as a global firm, with a Dow Latin America, Dow Europe, Dow Pacific, and other geographical divisions.

In May Gerstacker and his colleagues cause a sensation in world banking circles by chartering their own bank, the Dow Bank, in Switzerland; it is an immediate success

Is elected to the board of directors of the Hartford Insurance Group.

Is appointed chairman of the National Export Expansion Council by the Lyndon B. Johnson administration, a position he will occupy until 1973.

On 28 December is re-elected as chairman of the Michigan State Mental Health Society.

1966   Dow company becomes object of widespread campus protests against the war in Vietnam as the principal manufacturer of napalm. Gerstacker, who with Ted Doan becomes Dow's principal spokesman on this issue, achieves nationwide notoriety with frequent appearances on national TV, a heavy speech schedule, and virtually daily media interviews.

Establishes the Midland Law Enforcement Awards, made annually to outstanding officers of the Midland police and sheriff's organizations.

73

On 15 September testifies before the House Ways and Means Committee urging a general tax increase as an alternative to adoption of LBJ's proposed suspension of investment tax credit.

A bridge over the Rio Grande River in Texas, built to provide access to a fluorspar mine owned by Dow, is named the Carl A. Gerstacker International Bridge.

1967   On 29 March Secretary of Commerce John Connor presents to Gerstacker and other Dow officials the President's "E" Award for Excellence in Exporting.

Serves on a Michigan State Educational Panel asked to devise a plan for the development of higher education in Michigan over the next twenty years.

Receives Ohio Governor's Award as "an outstanding native son" who has contributed to the "advancement of the prestige of Ohio."

EVERYWHERE YOU LOOKED, AT THE END OF 1960, YOUTH was taking over. The old hands in government and industry were moving out, and the youngsters were moving in.

In Washington, Pres. Dwight D. Eisenhower, who was seventy, was being replaced by John F. Kennedy, aged forty-three. The oldest of the U.S. senators, Theodore F. Green, ninety-three, was succeeded by forty-two-year-old Claiborne Pell. The new governor of Michigan was John B. Swainson, who was thirty-five.

In industry the takeover by the young followed the same pattern. At the Ford Motor Company Robert S. McNamara, forty-four, was named the new president and Lee A. Iacocca, thirty-six, became general manager of the Ford Division. David Rockefeller, forty-five, became president of the Chase Manhattan Bank, the nation's second largest bank.[1]

At Dow Chemical Carl Gerstacker, forty-four, took over as the new board chairman from Earl W. Bennett, who was eighty, and Herbert D. (Ted) Doan, who was thirty-eight, became the executive vice president, succeeding Mark E. Putnam, seventy-four.

The changes at Dow were triggered when Dr. Putnam dropped dead of a heart attack on 6 November, during the same week John F. Kennedy was being elected to the U.S. presidency. Bennett, whose eyesight was beginning to fail, decided it was time to slow down, and he resigned as board chairman at age eighty, nominating Gerstacker to succeed to the position. (Afflicted with glaucoma, Bennett at that time could just barely make out the papers he was working with by holding them up close to his face.) He had already turned over the chairmanship of the Finance Committee to Gerstacker the year before. For the time being, Lee Doan stayed on as president and CEO, although he was already sixty-six.

The announcement of these changes left the Dow company buzzing with rumors. Who was going to succeed Lee Doan as chief executive? How long would he stay on after reaching sixty-five, the generally accepted retirement age? For the next few months the rumor mill operated at full blast. What only a few people in the top management knew was that Doan (with the help of Bennett and Putnam) had already picked his successor and was grooming him for the succession. His original selection for the new CEO of Dow had been William H. (Bill) Schuette, the forty-seven-year-old manager of the Michigan Division of the company (originally called the Midland Division), a brilliant student of modern management methods who had proved he could work effectively with older managers. This was important because a majority of Dow's major managers at the time were older than sixty-five.

Tragically, Schuette died suddenly of a heart attack on 8 November 1959, the day before Lee Doan's sixty-fifth birthday, and Doan was suddenly and unexpectedly back to square one in the search for a successor.

There was no dearth of candidates. There was Dutch Beutel, down in Texas, but his style was dictatorial—and even worse, Midlanders suspected he would try to move the Dow headquarters to Texas if he could. Tink Campbell was a candidate, but he was the only one who seemed to take his candidacy seriously. Ben Branch, the bright young manager of the Plastics Department, was forty-five and a rising star, but the older managers considered him too aggressive. Macauley Whiting, Schuette's successor in Midland, was only thirty-five. The field, therefore, rather quickly shook out to two leading contenders—Carl Gerstacker and Ted Doan.

For the next two years these two candidates duked it out in an amazingly long and gentlemanly exhibition as Lee Doan and the Dow board of directors watched at ringside, trying to

decide which of the two was the better candidate to be the next chief executive of the company.

"Probably in 1960, if you had had an election, Carl Gerstacker would have been [elected] president," Ted Doan said later.

In 1962 I was. The debate went on for two years, and the issue was never resolved, so they needed to have a vote [of the board of directors]. I think it was the first time in the history of the company that happened. There aren't many people that know to this day that that was a vote of the board. In other words, it was a disputed election rather than an appointment.

I think Gerstacker and I handled ourselves reasonably well, in the sense that we debated between the two of us all the way through this thing. We didn't upset the organization, we didn't cause a schism, and the thing came out the way it came out.

My father, Lee Doan, set up the organization. It was a dandy. Gerstacker was chairman and I was president and Branch was executive vice-president. He put all those people in place. I am convinced that Lee Doan was out selling me. I think he probably had great difficulty doing that. My suspicion is that he had previously indicated to Gerstacker that he would be president of the company. I think he had to make a switch of horses somewhere along there. I think Gerstacker handled that exceedingly well. I don't know how he handled it personally, but in terms of the effect on others, the way he handled himself was good.

I can lose gracefully. Carl can't. He doesn't want to lose one tennis game gracefully. I play tennis with him today, and he says, "My wife tells me I should learn to lose gracefully." And he's laughing like crazy because he knows that's the last thing he wants to do. So how he handled that as gracefully as he did, I don't know. Because he lost and Carl doesn't like losing. He's not used to losing.

Branch was aware of everything that was going on, and he was vociferously in favor of my becoming president. Why did Branch want me in there? The reasons are the same. I was very much an advocate of change and doing new things and trying to get on to new steps. I see Carl as a guy who does everything well and likes things once they get going, but is almost habitually an opponent of things until they get going. Rightly or wrongly, I thought he would be a good steward of assets, but not a builder, and Branch felt exactly the same way.

Branch was a builder first, last and always. Dutch Beutel was a builder. I was absolutely convinced that Dow had to have a builder mentality in there [as chief executive]. And the prime candidate, Carl, was in my opinion a steward rather than a builder. So, I did everything I could do ethically. And he as well. There was not one shred of bad business that I'm aware of done in the process of that two years. When that election occurred, and when the dust settled, Ben and Carl and I started working together.[2]

77

Gerstacker himself did not see it much differently. "I probably thought I should have been the chief executive instead of Ted, but I think part way through the experience, I began to believe that he was better than I would have been," he said. "Today, I think that he was better than I would have been. I would not have been as willing to have a triumvirate or troika, or to listen to other people as much as Ted did. I think he was actually better for the company. His willingness to use Branch and me made it a much better system than if I had been the chief executive or if Branch had been the chief executive officer. I think it is a great ability that Ted has that was well-used. That is an honest, sincere evaluation."[3]

There was no unanimity on the question. Paul Oreffice, Dow president and CEO from 1978 to 1987, said Gerstacker would have been a "great" CEO. "Ted Doan was always

encouraging and supportive of research and had many fine qualities," Oreffice said, "but Carl was by far the better businessman."[4]

Ben Branch later described how the three of them worked together to run the company. "We had what I thought then, and I think today, was the best management in American business," Branch said. "Ted was the president of the company. He was the one that set the philosophy of the company. Ted Doan invented the matrix system of management, which was awkwardly called 'the business concept' for lack of any other name. He implemented this business concept when he became president. Ted also handled the difficult political problems—not political in the sense of politics, but the problems that we were exposed to with napalm and that sort of thing.

78

> Carl [Gerstacker] was Mr. Outside. Carl was an absolute magician with the financial community. I think that Carl could get more mileage out of fewer numbers to prove Dow's greatness than any financial executive that I've ever known. He was also directly responsible for the marketing organization and for the purchasing organization. So, as I say, he was Mr. Outside.
>
> And I was Mr. Inside. My biggest job was to try to find projects that we could push to get the company in motion, and we supported some pretty sorry projects. But one of the wonderful characteristics of this company is that once the people came to understand that we really wanted to expand, why it came with a rush. It was really a troika. Ted was the leader. Carl was Mr. Outside, and I was Mr. Inside, and I think we did a damned good job.[5]

For the next decade or two, the three of them worked together like a beautifully synchronized watch. "We met almost daily," Branch said. "We had a hell of an intimate organization. Our offices were practically contiguous, and I

doubt that when we were in town there was a day passed that we didn't talk together about something."

Once a year the three of them went on a retreat together, invariably at the Caneel Bay resort on St. John in the U.S. Virgin Islands, and they would sit on the beach there most of the day with masses of papers, comparing notes on who in the company deserved or was ready for promotion, what major projects the company had coming along, and the biggest problems it was facing. By the time they were through they had mapped out and had agreed upon the major moves that the company would make in the year ahead, and which of the younger executives would be expected to lead them.

"The three of us would go down there and have a management meeting," Ted Doan said.

> Caneel Bay wasn't set up for management meetings, but with three people sitting there on the beach with a bunch of papers nobody knew what we were trying to do. In fact that was funny. People would come along and say, "We've seen you here for years. What are you doing? Are you writing a book?"
>
> We worked very hard on the people aspects of the company. We really got that organized. All those systems that are more or less used to today, we put together. We did the process of putting down probably the top 300 people in the company, and then kept working these lists over. We concentrated a hell of a lot on that, and the systems that we used to run these people. Some of these things have sort of worn themselves out. In fact, I've been advocating the last few years they dump some of those things. You know, they just get so embedded that they get destructive. They were damn good when they started. So that's the way that things ran. It ran pretty well and did OK.

It was in all probability the best three-man team ever to run a U.S. business.

MASTER OF CEREMONIES

The era following World War II was still the heyday of the testimonial dinner, an elaborate affair organized as a special event to pay tribute to some eminent person, usually for lifetime achievement. Gerstacker became an expert at organizing these events and a specialist in serving as toastmaster and master of ceremonies for them.

The first of these he organized was a salute to his mentor, Earl W. Bennett, which took place 18 January 1960, celebrating the old man's eightieth birthday and his sixty years of service with the Dow company. A heavy winter blizzard hit Midland that evening, and some of the New York financial moguls who were to have participated were stranded in airports somewhere, unable to get to Midland. Gerstacker read their messages in their stead at the actual event, relayed to him by one means or another.[6]

80

Earl Bennett continued to serve on the Dow board of directors and Finance Committee until March 1969, when he was eighty-nine; he died at the age of ninety-three. During his declining years, when he was totally blind, Gerstacker made sure he still played bridge. Carl knew how much the old man enjoyed the game, and would gather up a few of Bennett's friends and take them to his house for a few hands of bridge. One of the friends would sit on the arm of Bennett's chair and whisper in his ear what cards he had been dealt, and what cards were being played. Bennett would call for a card out of his hand and thus was able to play as well as, or perhaps even better than, a sighted person.

Another big testimonial affair over which Gerstacker presided was the seventieth birthday bash of Leland I. Doan on 9 November 1964. The headliner at this event was George Romney, who was being ballyhooed at the time as a potential presidential candidate. He had been elected to his second

term as governor of Michigan just five days earlier. "I'm here," Romney said, "because I admire Lee Doan." Doan responded by expressing the hope that Romney would become the next president of the United States. Also on hand were Dr. Harlan Hatcher, president of the University of Michigan, and Charles Allen Thomas, board chairman of Monsanto Chemical Company.[7]

Governor Romney was also the star at another of Gerstacker's big testimonial dinners on 7 February 1967—this one a tribute to Norman C. (Slim) Rumple, celebrating his thirty years as editor of the *Midland Daily News* and his election as president of the Michigan Press Association. Among the luminaries Gerstacker lined up to pay tribute to his friend Rumple were Frank Angelo, editor of the *Detroit Free Press*, Arthur E. Turner, founder and president of Northwood Institute (now Northwood University), and Prof. A. A. Applegate, head of the journalism department at Michigan State University, who as a young man had been Rumple's major professor at South Dakota State University.[8]

ECOLOGIST

The environmental "age" is generally agreed to have dawned with the publication of Rachel Carson's book, *Silent Spring*, in 1962. As a manufacturer of herbicides and pesticides, Dow Chemical was quickly involved in the debate and with the activists who took up Carson's crusade, and its board chairman was one of those who became thoroughly involved with the issue from its infancy.

Gerstacker's views on industrial pollution were quite straightforward—industry should concentrate on minimizing or even eliminating waste product, he said, thereby cutting down on the pollution problem at the same time it boosted

81

its own profits. The waste that industry threw away cost it money in at least two major ways: first, the waste that did not become salable product became one cost, and second, the cost of disposing of that waste became another. Focusing on eliminating the waste stream was the best thing to do—building big waste disposal facilities was costly and while a necessary expense of doing business should only be the solution of last resort. Many industries, he said, could actually improve their profits by working hard on eliminating their pollution.

In February of 1966, Pres. Lyndon B. Johnson sent a massive legislative program to the Congress aimed at cleaning up the nation's waters. "No unit of government or industry has the right to destroy America's heritage by polluting her lakes and streams," the president said in forwarding his proposals.

The Michigan Chamber of Commerce convened a one-day water pollution conference to discuss the subject in Lansing on 23 March, with Governor Romney and Carl Gerstacker as the main speakers. The sponsors expected perhaps 200 to attend the meeting, but 432 businessmen, municipal officials, and state legislators showed up, packing out the hall.

"The President's message is quite clear," Gerstacker told the conferees. "It's a mandate for industry to use drive, imagination and ingenuity to assume leadership in the anti-pollution field."

"There's no use burying our head in the sand," Governor Romney said. "We recognize that we have a problem in Michigan and we need federal-state-local-private assistance to win this fight." He added that while Michigan had taken a leadership role among the states in this field, "even we are barely getting started."

Dow was hailed as a shining example of enlightened management for its leadership in water pollution control efforts. E. S. (Bud) Shannon, manager of Dow's Midland waste pollution facilities, told the meeting that Dow had $8 million

invested in waste control facilities which required an annual expenditure of $2 million to operate.

"We are convinced that pollution control is part of the cost of doing business," Gerstacker said, "and I believe that any industry I know of in Michigan can control its pollution problems without spending itself out of business."

He advised business firms to establish a climate in which their employees were encouraged, and even rewarded, for finding new ways to control pollution. "Occasionally you will be surprised to find that such controls can be profitable by improving yields and reducing waste," he said. "Instead of trying to find out what to do with waste, try to find ways to stop it or stop it from occurring."[9]

The 1966 speech was only the beginning. For the remainder of his career, he would be asked to address the subject of the environment more than any other topic. His advice to industry to cut down on its waste in order to boost profits and minimize pollutants became known as "the Gerstacker approach" and is widely hailed as one of the soundest ways to deal with the problem.

As he told the Economic Club of Detroit in 1972,

I do believe with a passion in the profit motive, and I really believe that if we hitch the profit motive to some of our problems, we will get them solved. Pollution control will continue on forever if we see it simply as a drag on earnings, as a necessary nuisance, classified as overhead. If we see the opportunity in pollution and exploit that opportunity to the hilt, then we will help our earnings, and we will solve our pollution problems, and we will help solve the nation's pollution problems. But we need the profit incentive. Doing something simply because it's good citizenship isn't enough. It doesn't really motivate. So I urge you to harness the profit motive to your pollution problems. Try it. I think you'll like it.[10]

83

MR. OUTSIDE

Gerstacker moved smoothly into the role of "Mr. Outside." In one of his earliest interviews as board chairman he was asked by Emanuel Doernberg of the *New York American* what his goals were for the Dow company. Without missing a beat, he responded, "I'd like to see people in our company paid better than practically anyone else and I'd like to see our product prices down to a level where our customers would do better than practically anyone else." "Isn't that going to be a tough thing to do?" Doernberg asked. "Yes," said Gerstacker, "but I don't know why people working together can't achieve such ends."[11]

In contrast to Earl Bennett, who disliked public speaking intensely and very rarely delivered a formal talk during his sixty-nine-year career, the new board chairman soon became known as an excellent public speaker who always had a telling message, possessed an entertaining store of fresh jokes, and always seemed to enjoy himself in that role.

He planned fastidiously both the content and delivery of his major talks, and would work diligently on both of these elements, weeks and months ahead of time. As he traveled about the world he usually had with him the text of at least one talk that was "in process," and in a spare hour or two in a hotel room somewhere he would practice the talk before a mirror, polishing his gestures and timing and emphasis, over and over again. By the time he stood up to actually give the speech he was able to do it with little or no reference to the speech cards that he always carried. On the cards he would note places where he might (or might not) insert a joke, depending on how the audience was reacting to the talk, and which joke he wanted to insert in that spot if need be.

He knew a good joke could relax an audience and make it more receptive to his message, so he kept a store of basic

jokes that he used over and over again, perhaps eight or ten in all (he would drop a joke from this file if it wasn't "working," or add one, as time went by). They were jokes that he told and retold, time and again, from one town and audience to the next, and he was reasonably sure he could get a laugh with them. If they did not produce a laugh, he dropped them.

One that never failed him he called "the Mabel joke." He would say,

> I got into Pittsburgh (or Seattle, or whatever the city was) late last night, and by the time I got to my hotel room I was in no mood to go to sleep, so I looked around the room for some reading matter. Well, all I could find was a Gideon bible, stuck away in a drawer. So I opened it up, and I must say that you people are very thoughtful in this town. On the first page someone had written, "If you're having trouble sleeping, try reading the 23rd Psalm." I thought, Gee, that's a nice thought, and I turned to the next page and someone had written, "And if you're still having trouble sleeping, try reading the 13th chapter of Second Corinthians." And I thought, Gee, what nice people. And then I turned the next page, and in an entirely different handwriting someone had written, "And if you're still having trouble, hi there, my name is Mabel, and if you'll call me at 123-4567 I'll come right over."

85

He had an extraordinary ability to do complex mathematical calculations in his head while continuing a conversation. He would use this ability on occasion when a question came up from the audience that required serious calculation, as sometimes occurred when he was addressing financial groups. He would respond, "I'll have to figure out the answer to that, and I will, but while I'm doing it let's continue on with the questions." Two or three questions later he would come

back to the complex mathematical question and give his answer, having done the math in his head.

Success begets success. As he gained more and more skill as a speaker, he was sought out more and more frequently as a speaker.

As Dow Chemical expanded abroad he was called upon to give speeches in many countries, and he always made it a point to address an audience in its own language. At various times he gave talks in German, Spanish, Malay, Croat, Japanese, and other tongues, although he spoke none of those languages. *Nation's Business* magazine once asked him how he did it.

"It's no mystery," Gerstacker said with a grin. "I get the speech in English. Then we get an expert to translate it and record it on tape. Then I listen to the tape, write it out phonetically and just practice. It's a lot of work, but it's worth it."[12]

86

His first big dose of the national news limelight occurred on 21 June 1961 when he presided over the dedication of the Office of Saline Water's first seawater conversion plant at Freeport, Texas. It was also his first meeting with Lyndon B. Johnson, then vice president of the United States, who journeyed to Freeport to deliver the main address on this occasion. The plant was based on technology developed by Dow and was the first successful effort to make fresh water from salt.

Pres. John F. Kennedy, who was on crutches at the time and confined to the White House, decided the day before the event that he did not care to be upstaged by L.B.J. He set up a press show at the White House to which he invited L. I. Doan and A. P. Beutel of Dow. At the appointed time, before the assembled press, J. F. K. pressed a button that started the machinery working down in Texas and initiated the flow of fresh water through a special pipe.[13]

Meanwhile, down in Texas, Gerstacker and Texas Division general manager Earle Barnes were hosting L.B. J. and his wife Lady Bird and secretary of the interior Stewart Udall. They all applauded as fresh water gushed from a pipe after the president had pushed the button at the White House. L. B. J. then delivered his speech, and they applauded again. It was Gerstacker's first meeting with Johnson. That evening, following the dedication, the Johnsons put on one of their celebrated impromptu performances at a reception organized by the Democratic Party at the Riverside Country Club. "It was quite a show," Barnes said later.

REORGANIZING THE COMPANY

During the first two years of its reign the troika did a lot of traveling around the world—especially Ted Doan—talking to Dow employees and taking the pulse of the company. By the fall of 1964 the three men had decided what needed to be done, and they set about reorganizing the company. It had sprouted branches and subsidiaries all over the world in the dozen years preceding, but still had the organization and mindset of a small midwestern American company. The most pressing basic need, therefore, was to transform Dow into a truly global enterprise, one that was organized as a global firm and viewed itself as a global enterprise.

87

In order to get the company's board of directors thinking in these terms, Gerstacker led the board over to Europe for its meeting in November 1964. Surprisingly, a majority of the board members had never been outside of North America before. The board meeting itself took place in Zurich, at Dow's European headquarters, and the board then made stops to meet with local officials and industrialists in Zurich, Paris, Amsterdam, and London. It was the first time

the board had met outside the United States, and in retrospect clearly marked the coming-of-age of Dow Chemical as a world entity.

A month or two later, at their annual midwinter sojourn on the beach at St. John, the troika honed the details of the reorganization it had in mind and refined its plans for putting it into effect. The men then convened a "global management meeting" for 16–18 March 1965, on the campus of Michigan State University, East Lansing, Michigan, for about seventy of the top Dow executives from around the world, at which they would lay out their intentions and ask for counsel and assistance.

Their main objective was to decentralize the Dow company out of Midland and set up control organizations around the world closer to the day-to-day activities of the firm. The organization in Europe was to be upgraded to become Dow Europe, and the organization in Latin America was to become Dow Latin America. Dow Canada was already in place. The vast area in Asia was to be organized to become Dow Pacific, with headquarters in Hong Kong. The U.S. operations were to be reorganized and divided into two organizations, a Dow USA and a Dow corporate headquarters. All these geography-based organizations, called "area headquarters," would report to the corporate headquarters in Midland but retain a large share of autonomy in their own spheres of control. Although they had been in the vanguard of the firm's rapid growth in the world, Dow International and Dow Inter-American would now fade from existence entirely.

Macauley Whiting, as the president of Dow International, was given the honor of introducing the general plan of reorganization. As it turned out, there was a job in the new, reshaped organization for everyone except Whiting. "I had in one quick stroke done myself out of the best job in the company," Whiting said later. "Nobody else had as much

authority and as little responsibility."[14] (Eventually, Whiting took on a newly created position as the company's energy czar.)

Gerstacker followed Whiting's presentation with a discussion of the new role of management in this kind of organization. "Unless those of us at our level who are responsible for the Dow company do some changing, unless we set the example and show the way, there is probably going to be a lot of talk but very little actual change taking place," he said. "Unless we make some changes ourselves the new view we are taking of the Dow organization is just going to be a paper view, and not much of a success." The board of directors, he said, would become a sort of traffic cop. "When a matter arrives at the board level, the decision will really already have been made, and the details worked out [at the geographical headquarters level]," he said. "The function of the Board in this kind of operation will be to set the direction. The Board will approve an authorization or a project on the basis chiefly of whether it is moving us in the right direction."

89

He said the board would "provide a green light as long as the project goes in the right direction, and the Board will turn on the red light and bring to a screeching halt anything that runs counter to the direction we have decided to follow." In general, the heads of the geographic regions would be members of the board and would be bringing projects from their regions to the board for final approval.

The company's Executive Committee would concern itself less and less with the details of various projects and more and more with direction. The Finance Committee, he said, would change little because it was already geared to worldwide operation, having been forced in that direction by events. The individual top managers, he admitted, would make mistakes. "We cannot reform ourselves completely overnight," he said. "Some of you will push us in the direction of being a world-wide company, and others of you will

have to be pulled yourselves in this direction. I leave it to each of you whether you want to push us, or whether you want us to push you."

The top managers of the company, he said (meaning himself and Ted Doan and Ben Branch), would increasingly be planners rather than doers. "I speak for Ben and Ted as well as myself," he said, "when I tell you that we are here to see this new system work, and we mean to see that it does work, and we promise you a continuing, concerted effort to make it work."[15]

The succeeding years were crowned with success as the Dow company continued by leaps and bounds to grow and prosper, and the reshaping of the company the three of them effected in 1965 was to remain essentially unchanged for the next thirty years.

90   ## EXPORT PROMOTER

In 1965 Gerstacker had a telephone call from John Connor, an old friend from the chemical industry who had become Lyndon Johnson's secretary of commerce. Connor had been board chairman of Allied Chemical Corporation before going to Washington. The president, Connor said, wanted to nominate Gerstacker as chairman of the National Export Expansion Council (NEEC), an organization he had formed to promote greater exports by American industry. Connor did not say whether L.B.J. remembered Gerstacker from their meeting in Texas a few years before, but he did urge him to accept the nomination. "We have got to stop the dollar drain, Carl, and we don't think anyone else can do as good a job as you can," he said.

If he had known the job would last eight years—from 1966 through the end of 1973—Gerstacker might well have

turned it down, but "I felt like I'd been called to the service again," he said, and he accepted L.B.J.'s summons. His role as the principal U.S. promoter of exports abroad became possibly his single most significant contribution to the nation but at the same time one of the least recognized by the general public.

The "dollar drain" that Connor referred to—the U.S. balance of payments deficit—was one of the most complex problems the country faced and at the time the subject of a raging controversy between economists and financiers and politicians. Just how much of a threat was the drain to the U.S. economy, or was it no threat at all? Both sides of the question had their partisans. "Because of its very complexity [the problem] is little understood," Gerstacker said, "and because it is so little understood it is difficult to stir people to action about it."[16]

His task, as he saw it, was exactly that—"to stir people to action about it."

The problem, as he analyzed it, was simply that the United States was sending far more dollars out of the country than were flowing back into it. For example, the war in Vietnam represented a huge outflow. American tourists in their travels abroad spent at least double the amount that foreign tourists brought to the United States. The U.S. foreign aid program was another major factor. And finally there was the trade imbalance, with more and more foreign products being sold in the United States and lower and lower volumes of U.S. goods being sold abroad.

The answer, as simply as he could put it, was that American manufacturers needed to mount a major effort to sell their products abroad, and that was the message he carried across the nation for the next eight years. "Somehow we have to match the outflow of dollars with a greater inflow," he said, "or face the impairment of the dollar and of our economic structure."

91

The Commerce Department organized regional export expansion councils (REECs) composed of business leaders in the major cities and these became a focal point for the campaign to boost American exports. National committees were set up under the aegis of NEEC to study various aspects of the problem and make recommendations to the administration. There was a Tax Committee—Gerstacker saw that as being so important that he became its chairman—and an Export Finance Committee and a committee on ocean transport and freight rates.

The local councils would hold one- or two-day meetings to discuss exports in their area or industry, and Gerstacker would fly in to deliver a keynote address or a major tub-thumping message at these events.

The whole program was designed to call attention to the opportunities and benefits of export, and it led many companies to initiate export departments and programs for the first time. Gerstacker liked to cite the case of a tiny, eight-employee firm in Memphis, Tennessee, which manufactured bakers' mitts and had never even thought of exporting its product before. Its mitts became so popular abroad that it soon had to double its workforce. "If Memphis can do it," Gerstacker said, "you can do it too."

It helped a great deal that the U.S. chemical industry was one of the leaders in producing a positive balance of payments. In 1973, Gerstacker's last year as NEEC leader, the U.S. chemical industry exported about $5.4 billion worth of product, compared to imports into the United States of $2.4 billion.

A succession of honors came to Gerstacker and the Dow company as a result of his export work. On 29 March 1967, Secretary Connor presented Gerstacker and other Dow officials the president's "E" Award for Excellence in Exporting, and in 1971 the Nixon administration gave Gerstacker the first "E" Award conferred upon an individual by that

administration. Nixon's secretary of commerce, Maurice H. Stans, who presented the award, noted that Gerstacker had served as the government's export expansion leader under both Democratic and Republican administrations, and that the nation's exports had grown from $16.5 billion in 1965, when he took over, to more than $42 billion in 1970.

On 13 December 1973, as his term of office was running out, Gerstacker was called to Washington for a private luncheon at the Department of Commerce. There the secretary of commerce, Frederick B. Dent, conferred upon him the Department of Commerce Special Medal for "important contributions to improving the economic strength of the United States through the expansion of exports." Under his "dynamic and effective leadership," the citation said, "many businessmen and other civic-spirited citizens throughout the nation, as members of the Export Expansion Councils, have shared generously their international business experience and expertise with Government and with their fellow citizens. His dedicated and constructive service is an outstanding example of business participation in programs benefiting the interests of our country."

93

The nation, said the secretary, had been "well served" by Gerstacker's work.[17]

NAPALM

In 1965, an opinion research poll asking people about their knowledge of the chemical industry revealed that at that time only thirty-eight percent of the public had ever heard of the Dow Chemical Company. Four years later that number had zoomed all the way up to ninety-one percent—extremely high, about the same percentage able to identify the occupant of the White House at any given time. The factor that brought

Dow so urgently and powerfully to the world's attention in that four-year span was a product called "napalm." U.S. troops were using it in the Vietnam War and it became one of the chief focuses of the worldwide protests against that war. Napalm, which Dow began making rather by accident, transformed Dow in a short time from a company virtually unknown to the general public to one of the most famous.

Napalm, a form of liquid fire more correctly known as napalm B, was developed by the U.S. Army in 1964. It was a simple mixture of fifty percent polystyrene, twenty-five percent benzene, and twenty-five percent gasoline, made by what chemists call "bathtub chemistry"—just mix up the ingredients, and you've got it. It was highly useful to the military in Vietnam, where the enemy guerrillas operated from holes and concealments of all types. "Napalm, by virtue of its splashing and spreading, can get into such defensive positions," explained Gen. Earle G. Wheeler, chairman of the U.S. Joint Chiefs of Staff. "It's also especially effective against antiaircraft positions, because normally the enemy digs a hole—a protected position—and puts his machine down in the hole. . . . It takes a direct hit with high explosives in order to destroy it. The napalm splashes in and incapacitates the crew and sometimes destroys the weapon."[18]

Dow was one of seventeen U.S. producers of polystyrene that the Department of Defense asked to submit bids to make napalm in 1965 (polystyrene being the principal ingredient), and the DOD then awarded contracts to five of these firms to make it, including Dow. Dow set up a small mixing line at its Torrance, California, plant to fulfill its contract, manned by a crew of ten. It was such a minor piece of business—Dow never made more than $5 million worth of napalm in any single year—that when the protests began, Gerstacker, Doan, and Branch were not even aware that their company was making the material.

The protests against napalm, which it was alleged the U.S. military forces were using recklessly and indiscriminately in Vietnam and killing women and children, began on the West Coast in March 1966. War protesters lay down on the railroad tracks in Redwood City, California, attempting to prevent shipments of napalm by UTC (United Technology Center, a subsidiary of United Aircraft Corporation). In April Witco Chemical, another producer, faced protesters at its annual meeting in New York.

When the Dow annual meeting convened in Midland in mid-May, Gerstacker and his colleagues also expected pickets, and Gerstacker drew up a position statement on napalm that he put in his pocket in case he needed it—but none showed up. This statement, which he and the company were to use extensively over the succeeding years, said the following:

> The Dow Chemical Company endorses the right of any American to protest legally and peacefully an action with which he does not agree.
>
> Our position on the manufacture of napalm is that we are a supplier of goods to the Defense Department and not a policy maker. We do not and should not try to decide military strategy or policy.
>
> Simple good citizenship requires that we supply our government and our military with those goods which they feel they need whenever we have the technology and capability and have been chosen by the government as a supplier.
>
> We will do our best, as we always have, to try to produce what our Defense Department and our soldiers need in any war situation. Purely aside from our duty to do this, we will feel deeply gratified if what we are able to provide helps to protect our fighting men or to speed the day when fighting will end.

The protesters' highly publicized war against Dow began on the East and West Coasts simultaneously on 28 May 1966. That day the Dow offices in Rockefeller Center were besieged by about seventy-five protesters representing various New York City peace groups who handed out leaflets urging the bystanders to boycott Saran Wrap and other Dow products. On the West Coast, at the Torrance plant, more than 100 pickets showed up, organized by Students for a Democratic Society (SDS), the leading student antiwar group.

These boisterous but nonviolent protests made a big splash on national TV, and for the next few years the antiwar protests against Dow were a regular drumbeat, occurring most often on major college campuses. During the next four school years, Dow was to become the target of 221 disturbances of varying violence, the usual object of these protests being the Dow recruiter visiting campuses to recruit employees.

The other chemical companies supplying napalm quickly dropped out of the picture. Gerstacker and his colleagues on the Dow board, on the other hand, decided to stick it out. The company had a long tradition of supplying the military with the products it needed in time of war, and it was not about to change its stripes because of the anti-Vietnam War marchers. At the same time, however, it had never experienced such blind, determined opposition to its policies. The protests continued to increase in frequency and fury. Some of the company's board of directors began to talk about "getting out of it." "The military ought to make its own napalm," they grumbled. Key executives such as Gerstacker and Doan were spending virtually all their time on the napalm issue.

In March 1967 the matter came up for a yes or no decision by the Dow board. Gerstacker opened that meeting by calling for a full discussion of the napalm question. "I told them we might not be aware of how much controversy there was about the moral and ethical considerations involved and

that we should discuss whether we should continue or modify our supply of napalm," he said.

The meeting went on for two days, with several adjournments. During the adjournments the directors talked to each other in small groups, or talked to other people in the company, or to friends, neighbors, clergymen. Gerstacker himself huddled with his good friend the Reverend Theodore M. Greenhoe of the Memorial Presbyterian Church in Midland.

"It was a very open debate," Ted Doan said. "There were no set positions. Frequently the board broke into small groups for very intense discussion. Members talked back and forth. At the end of the first day, with nothing firmly decided, but with three or four members looking as if they might take a stand against napalm, everyone went home and must have had a very troubled sleep. The next morning each of these men individually came to my office and said that after careful and troubled consideration they agreed that the company should continue what it was doing. I am not sure of any exceptions on the board today (1968); maybe one at most."[19]

97

"Our sons were serving in that war, and we felt a strong obligation to support them," Gerstacker said. Once the Dow board of directors had decided that the company would "stand up for what it believed in," the debate within the company was over. The company would do what it perceived as its duty to its country.

Throughout this period Gerstacker and Doan continued to be the principal spokespersons for the company and frequently appeared together, as they did more than once on the NBC *Today Show*. Both were fair game for the press during this time, and Gerstacker on occasion was tackled by interviewers who literally leaped out of the shrubbery, occasionally with microphones and camera crews, as he was approaching the building that was his destination. "Has Dow decided to stop making napalm yet? Why not?" they would ask. "Are you

willing to talk about the obscene profits Dow is making from napalm? Does the government give you figures on how many Vietnamese babies they've killed with napalm? Do you ask for those numbers?" Gerstacker would patiently respond that the use of napalm was a military decision, not the company's, that it was a small item—amounting to less than one-quarter of one percent of Dow sales—and that the profits from it were even less than that. He would also add that the government was reassuring Dow that the product was being used with great discretion.

Time would bear him out. In the end the accusations of napalm misuse turned out to be fabrications. Highly qualified medical doctors such as Howard A. Rusk, medical editor of the *New York Times,* H. Charles Scharnweber of Dow Medical, and a great many others, went to Vietnam during this period to check on the women and children purportedly killed with napalm, and could not find any such cases. The frequent burn cases they encountered during the investigations were caused by careless or ignorant use of gasoline, they found.[20]

During the 1967–68 school year—the antiwar protests peaked, it will be remembered, in that "crazy" spring of 1968—campus incidents involving Dow occurred virtually daily. In response, the company began publishing an internal publication called *Napalm News* to inform key executives and personnel about where such events were occurring, who from Dow was on the scene, and the steps being taken to cope with what was expected. The first issue of the paper appeared in 8 November 1967, and the last on 25 March 1969.

The Dow annual meeting of 1968—these meetings had been held for many years at the Central Intermediate School in Midland, which had the largest auditorium in town—was in many respects the culmination of these events. The Dow meeting occurred in the middle of that tumultuous spring, midway between the assassination of Martin Luther King on

4 April and that of Sen. Robert F. Kennedy on 5 June. The so-called "March on Midland" was advertised months ahead of time on campuses and in the peace movement, and on 8 May about 300 students and activists converged on Midland (500 by some accounts), led by the Reverend Richard R. Fernandez of Clergy and Laymen Concerned About Vietnam (CALCAV). The New York–based CALCAV organized the event.

Doan and Gerstacker met with Fernandez and four of his colleagues for a long, fiery discussion at the Memorial Presbyterian Church, just across the street from the school, before as many spectators as could jam into the hall.

Meanwhile the lawn in front of the school had become a kind of slogan-chanting carnival, with discussion groups, amateur musical soloists and groups of various kinds, antiwar posters and picket signs. Across the street from them marched a counter-picketing group that supported Dow, including a young man who said he had just returned from the war in Vietnam and carried a sign saying "I Back Dow, I Like My V.C. Well Done."

Amazingly, no police were called. "Marching through a line of police to get to the meeting smacks of the police state," Gerstacker said, "and I don't think it's beneficial to the stockholders or to the company." The stockholders, 1,150 of them, calmly made their way through the pickets and filed into the meeting.

Gerstacker instituted a new rule at that meeting to control the lengthy, never-ending speeches to which the antiwar movement was devoted. It became known as "the Gerstacker rule" and is still used today at Dow's annual meeting of stockholders, and sometimes on other occasions. It posits that "if it takes more than five minutes to ask it, it's not a question but a speech, and if it takes more than five minutes to answer it, it's not an answer but a speech; and either one will be gaveled down." (In later years the time was slimmed down to

three minutes each for a question or an answer, and a large visible clock was installed in the stage area to tick off the time.)

One by one a dozen of the protesters took the microphone to ask questions, each of which Gerstacker answered himself. Two young men from Purdue tried to take over the microphone for a rambling discourse and were roundly booed. "My main problem," Gerstacker said, "was to try to restrain the employees and local people who wanted to throw these people out physically."[21]

He reserved the final word for himself. Addressing the protester group directly, Gerstacker told them: "You can harass us. You can hurt us—and we already have been hurt. You can intimidate us. We won't strike back because we respect your right to dissent. But as long as our democratically elected government sends draftees to die in Vietnam, we're going to support these men." The meeting ended in prolonged applause for Gerstacker and the stockholders filed out. Out on the lawn the picket groups were singing "We Shall Overcome."

As the war and the protests wound down, Gerstacker paused to review the situation in a speech to the New York Financial Writers. "During the napalm demonstrations against Dow I wanted very badly to go on a tour of the nation's campuses to tell our story, to respond to the student pleas, to explain why we felt we ought to continue to make napalm," he said. "But a still, small voice in my heart told me that if I did that, there would be a strong probability of great commotion on those campuses, high emotions, student groups opposing my views and student groups favoring them, and confrontations in which very possibly some people—perhaps a great many—would be hurt. So I did not go on any tour of the campuses, much as I wanted to."

I have been personally involved with student protests, however, particularly at a couple of small colleges with which I have some association, and in each case I have found this to be a stimulating and rewarding experience. The key to this kind of confrontation, I think, is to demonstrate your willingness to come to grips with whatever issues the students want to discuss. You have to be a superbly patient listener. Students will speak to you from ignorance, from emotion, often with flawed logic, and these are things we also suffered from at their age, but the times were different and a generation ago we weren't allowed to demonstrate our ignorance and our lack of logic as freely as we permit today . . . .You must be willing to admit that it's just possible that you might be wrong, and you ought to be willing to show that you've given that possibility some thought—and that you're willing to give their propositions some thought as well.

He distinguished carefully between two types of students, however. "I speak of those serious students, the majority of students, who earnestly want to carry on dialogue with representatives of business and government, not of those in the highly radical minority whose sole aim is the destruction of the university and the system and whose minds are closed to anything and everything you may say," he said. "We have always avoided debate or discussion under the auspices of the Students for a Democratic Society or any other group that believes in violence."

A lot of strange things happened to Dow people during the napalm disturbances. "Our recruiters have been locked up in their recruiting rooms many times," he said. "The collegiate record for that is still held by Harvard, by the way, at nine hours; our people have been robbed of their papers and briefcases and other belongings; sometimes they've had to leave by the back door, and once or twice they've had to escape by leaping out of a window; we've had a number of

101

bomb threats, and two actual bombings; but during all of this we have never had any Dow employee suffer actual physical harm—at least none worse than being spit upon, although I'm sure that's bad enough."[22]

HIT LIST

The Vietnam era also carried the threat of physical danger for Gerstacker and other Dow executives. A Charles Manson disciple, Sandra Good, phoned Gerstacker at his home on 4 September 1975, to inform him that he was on the Manson mass murder group's "hit list" of seventy-four U.S. businessmen who were to be executed by a "People's Court of Retribution." Good was a roommate of Lynette "Squeaky" Fromme, later convicted of attempting to assassinate President Gerald Ford. "Dow Chemical has wreaked havoc with the lives of thousands of people in Vietnam and in the United States," she declared. Gerstacker, she told the *Midland Daily News*, "was responsible for killing people and polluting the environment. They [Dow] have manufactured napalm, and everyone knows what napalm has done."

It was one of several such calls that he received. "They scared the socks off me," he said. "A death threat really gets your attention."[23]

His daughter Bette remembered an occasion about this time when she was approached by a stranger at a Midland student hangout called Tony's. "I'm told you're Carl Gerstacker's daughter," the young man said. "True," she replied. "Would you give him this?" requested the stranger, and he gave her an envelope full of anti-Dow literature. "It said stuff like that Saran Wrap was responsible for a lot of pregnancies, and stuff like that," Bette said. "I took it home and gave it to Dad. He took one look at it and he said, 'Where is this guy? I want to

talk to him.' We went tearing back to Tony's, but the fellow had disappeared."[24]

One of Gerstacker's favorite stories about the napalm era concerned a Dow recruiter who was interviewing candidates at a California school. Students were lined up in the hallway waiting to see him to interview for Dow jobs. In the interview booth next to him, meanwhile, was the recruiter for Standard of California, who had no interviews at all. The Standard recruiter worked on his papers awhile, and nothing happened; and when he had stood it as long as he could he went out and addressed the students in the hallway waiting to interview with Dow. "Gentlemen," he said, "I think you ought to know that we at Standard of California supply the gasoline to Dow Chemical that it uses to make napalm. Now, wouldn't some of you like to interview with me?"

That, Gerstacker said, "may be the ultimate compliment to those of us who have learned to live with confrontation."

103

RELATIONS WITH RUSSIA

Gerstacker rarely had reason to visit the Soviet Union, and only once did he stay there long enough to do any sightseeing and get a feel for the place. In 1959 he had contracted with the Russians to buy $13.5 million worth of benzene for Dow when it was in serious shortage in the United States—a transaction approved by the U.S. government—and it had been an unpleasant experience. He had been bitterly accused by American arch-conservatives of "dealing with the devil," even though the purchase kept American chemical plants operating. Doing business with the Soviets in those iron-curtain days was generally frowned upon by the American public. When Gerstacker returned from the Soviet Union in February 1967, after his only stay of any length in

the country, he told the press that he was very much in favor of Pres. Lyndon Johnson's policy of "loosening up" trade relations with the Soviets.

"Travel back and forth by people is very essential for understanding," Gerstacker said. "We have got to communicate, or we are going to have trouble. I favor any such effort as the President's and the State Department's 'building bridges to the East' program. I favor more East-West trade."

In preparation for his Russian trip he had read *The Penkovskiy Papers* (a book by turncoat Soviet spy Oleg Penkovskiy describing the USSR spy system), and to his astonishment the interpreter he was assigned in Moscow turned out to be one of the major spies mentioned in the book. Gerstacker asked this spy/interpreter why it was that he could ride in the Moscow subway, speaking English, and no one would pay any attention to him. "Moscow is a big city with people from many countries visiting all the time, and we pay no attention to them," said the interpreter. "Right now at your hotel, for example, there are two Canadians who arrived Tuesday, and three Englishmen who arrived Wednesday."

Gerstacker noted, "He didn't seem to realize the spying implications."[25]

6

CHAIRMAN OF THE BOARD, 1968–76

1968   On 24 May is named to a U.S. Chamber of Commerce "Special Commission to Consider the Problems of the Dollar."

On 12 June begins a one-year term as board chairman of the Manufacturing Chemists Association.

1969   Marriage with Jayne ends in divorce. Moves to a "bachelor pad" in Midland.

Is a delegate to the national conference of UNESCO (United Nations Educational, Scientific and Cultural Organization) in San Francisco, 23–25 November.

1970   Is elected a director of Carrier Corporation. Is now chairman of the executive committee of Dow Corning Corporation and a director of National City Bank of Cleveland and of Dundee Cement Company, Dundee, Michigan.

1971   Is recipient of the first "E" Award to an individual conferred by the Nixon administration for his contributions to the nation's export expansion efforts, having served as chairman of the National Export Expansion Council (NEEC) under both Democratic and Republican presidents.

Ted Doan retires as president and CEO of Dow and is succeeded by C. B. (Ben) Branch. Gerstacker continues as chairman.

1972   Achieves a lifelong dream and becomes owner of a stand of redwood trees in California, near Mendocino.

1973   On 2 March is elected chairman of the Advisory Council on Japan–U.S. Economic Relations, formed by the Nixon administration to advise it on U.S. economic policy vis-à-vis Japan. The council comprises fifty board chairmen and presidents representing a cross section of American business and works closely with a Japanese counterpart, the Japan-U.S. Economic Council. Gerstacker has been vice chairman of the council since its establishment in 1971.

In December is honored with the Department of Commerce Special

Medal, presented at a private luncheon at the Department of Commerce. His eight years of service as chairman of NEEC come to a close at year-end.

On 26 December is named to the Rockefeller University Council.

1974 In February is appointed to a three-year term as member of the Joint Committee on U.S.–Japan Cultural and Educational Cooperation by Secretary of State Henry Kissinger.

On 12 April appears on Merv Griffin show with entertainer Danny Thomas. Videotape of the show becomes a model used for years to train businessmen to make effective TV appearances.

On 20 June is chosen to receive the 1974 Chemical Industry Medal by the Society of Chemical Industry "in recognition of conspicuous service to applied chemistry."

Is now a trustee and vice chairman of the United Presbyterian Foundation, a member of the International Advisory Council of the Chase Manhattan Bank, and a director of Eaton Corporation.

During visit to West Coast is stricken with Legionnaires' Disease and spends several weeks fighting for his life at a clinic in Ft. Bragg, California. A young Ft. Bragg doctor cares for him and saves his life.

On 18 October is named "Midwestern Man of the Year" by the Drug, Chemical and Allied Trades Association (DCAT).

107

1975 His mother, Eda, dies at the age of ninety, having spent the declining years of her life in senility.

On 8 March marries Esther Little Schuette, widow of his close colleague and fellow Dow board member William H. Schuette (deceased in 1959), in a ceremony at St. John's Episcopal Church, Midland. Acquires three new stepchildren: Sandra, Gretchen, and William D. Schuette.

On 4 September receives death threat from a member of the Manson group.

On 19 November Michigan governor William Milliken names a seven-member bipartisan Michigan Efficiency Task Force, including Gerstacker,

and asks it to recommend a method of analyzing state government efficiency and costs.

Elevated to 33rd degree Mason at Scottish Rite Cathedral, Bay City, Michigan.

1976   On 5 May, at Dow's annual meeting of stockholders, announces his retirement as chairman of the board. Branch succeeds him as board chairman and Zoltan Merszei, a charismatic Hungarian, becomes the new president and CEO of Dow. Gerstacker remains a director and chairman of the Finance Committee until his sixty-fifth birthday in 1981.

108

IN THE FALL OF 1968 GERSTACKER'S FAMILY LIFE WENT smash. And like Humpty Dumpty falling off the wall, it was a complete smash, and could not be put together again. The more successful he became in his career, it seemed, the more of his time that career consumed, and the less time he had to devote to his wife and daughters, and the more his home life deteriorated. A final rupture with Jayne had been coming on for years now, and the breakup finally occurred that fall in spite of his best efforts to prevent it.

He avoided a divorce as long as he could. Divorce was against his basic principles and those of his parents.

Early in his marriage it had become clear that Jayne suffered from severe mental problems, and that these were compounded by, or were closely related to, recurring drinking problems. She was an alcoholic. She was given to severe bouts of depression, which led her to drink, and eventually to require institutionalization, not once or twice, but chronically.

In the family it was said that "Mom is sick," and she was "sick" a good deal of the time.[1]

"The entire time I was in the fifth and sixth grade she was being cared for in a place over in Wisconsin," his daughter Bette said, "and on the weekends my father would take Lisa and me and we would drive over to see Mom in Wisconsin."

"My mother," Bette said, "was a woman who needed a lot of attention, she was starving for attention and affection, and my father was not very demonstrative, didn't display his affection. She was a very loving person, generous to a fault, but she was an alcoholic, and when she drank she got nasty. They kept trying to treat her by sedating her. In fact at one time or another they tried just about everything on her, including electric shock treatments, but nothing worked."

Jayne tried to commit suicide several times, unsuccessfully. Gerstacker told a close friend about one occasion when he woke up in the middle of the night and found Jayne standing over him with a knife in her hand. He became active in both state and national mental health organizations, looking for answers, but did not find any that worked.

"She was a very beautiful woman when she was young," Bette said. "There was a story, I don't know if it's true, that my father was playing golf the first time he saw her—she was playing with some other people on the course—and he said to the people with him, 'There's my future wife.'"

In addition, Bette was turning out to be an intractable and rebellious child. Tucked away among Gerstacker's 1963 papers as board chairman was a clipping from *Parents' Magazine* entitled, "Why Kids Rebel." Bette, who was twelve at the time, says, "I'm sure that was for me."[2]

"One of the most vivid memories of my childhood is of a terrible spanking my father gave me when I was about twelve," she said. "I thought I was old enough to wear makeup but my folks didn't, and I went into the ladies locker room at the

country club one day and stole somebody's makeup kit. Of course when they saw me wearing makeup my folks wanted to know where I got it, and when they found out I'd stolen it my father turned me over his knee and gave me a spanking, and a good one—ten or twenty swats with full arm swing. Wow! I still remember it. And then my Dad took me and went with me to take the stuff back to the people it belonged to. That was pretty tough for a twelve-year-old kid. There were only a few times that he spanked me, but I'll never forget them, and today I think they're a good thing for a child who seriously misbehaves."

By the time the divorce decree became final in January 1969, Gerstacker had long since moved out of the big house on Main Street where they were living into what he called a "bachelor pad" on Bayliss Street—a small apartment with a living room, bedroom, and bathroom. There the chairman of the board subsisted, when he was home, on the only foods he knew how to cook—boiled hot dogs, which he loved and enjoyed (if necessary, every day of the week), boiled eggs, and chocolate brownies, which he either bought or got someone to make for him. At the time there was a Nabisco cookie made of chocolate and marshmallow called "Pinwheels," and he kept at least twenty packs of Pinwheels in his freezer so that he would not run out. Esther remembered, too, that he put salt on everything—hot dogs, Pinwheels, eggs, chicken—even, if he had one, in beer.

BETTE

With the divorce clock ticking, Jayne decided to take the girls on an extended vacation to Hawaii toward the end of 1968. Lisa, who was fourteen, liked Hawaii a great deal, but Bette, eighteen and a senior in high school, fell head over heels in love with it. The carefree life of a beachcomber, the idyllic

The identical Uhinck twins, Elsa and Eda, c. 1902. Eda was Carl's mother; Elsa (Pardee) was his "Auntie."

Eda Gerstacker, c. 1960.

Rollin M. (Rollie) Gerstacker, Carl's father. Sketch by his brother-in-law, Robert Uhinck, who changed the name to Ewing when he moved to California.

Elsa and James Pardee, Carl's aunt and uncle, 1936.

Carl as high school senior, 1933.

Carl graduates from University of Michigan, 1938.

Presentation of first 37-mm anti-tank gun to army by Duplex Printing Press Co., Battle Creek, Michigan, summer 1940. Gerstacker is second lieutenant at left.

Willard H. Dow, Dow Chemical CEO 1930–49, who took it upon himself to "sell" young Gerstacker to his colleagues, 1946.

Earl W. Bennett, Dow's legendary financial genius, who became Gerstacker's mentor.

Carl and his new bride, Jayne Harris, about to leave for a honeymoon in Hawaii, October 1950.

Wedding photograph of Elsa Gerstacker, Carl's sister, who married William W. Allen, 1936.

William W. Allen, 1936.

The "troika." C. Benson (Ben) Branch, left, was executive vice president, then president of Dow Chemical Company 1970–76; Carl Gerstacker was chairman of the board, 1960–76; and H. D. (Ted) Doan, right, was president and CEO, 1962–70. They ran the company jointly throughout this period.

Lisa Gerstacker, Carl's younger daughter and her family, 2002—Sean Walsh, husband, and Katie, their daughter.

Bette Gerstacker, Carl's elder daughter, and her children, daughter Nohea and son Kaena, 1979.

Carl marries Esther Little Schuette, St. John's Episcopal Church, Midland, 1975. (l to r) Gretchen Schuette, Sandra Schuette Joys, Esther, Carl, and William D. Schuette.

Board of Trustees, Rollin M. Gerstacker Foundation, 2002. (l to r) 1st row: Frank Gerace, Esther Gerstacker, Lisa Gerstacker, E. N. Brandt, Gail Allen Lanphear, and Mary McDonough (Administrative Assistant). 2nd row: Paul F. Oreffice, Alexio Baum, Jean Popoff, William S.Stavropoulos, William D. Schuette, Thomas Ludington, and Alan W. Ott.

weather, the intriguingly different Hawaiian culture and way of life, swept her off her feet. She was coming of age in the late 1960s at the height of the flower child culture, and Hawaii suited her lifestyle very well. She did not even go back to Michigan to finish the final credits for her high school diploma, but got her GED. She spent the next ten years in Hawaii, and eventually made Hawaii her permanent home. She lives in Hawaii today and is a grandmother.

"I was the rebel of the house, always was," Bette said. "I think there were basically two reasons I stayed in Hawaii. First, there was the warm weather. I never liked the cold in Michigan and the Hawaiian weather suited me just fine, always has. Second, and perhaps more important, I was running away. I didn't really realize it at the time, but I was running away, just wanted to get away. I was a lonely child much of the time. Mom was sick and Dad was gone."

Bette married a Hawaiian boy, Joseph Leong, a couple of years after her arrival there, and had a daughter, Nohea. When Nohea was about one year old, Bette tried cocaine and was a user for the next ten years. She divorced Leong in 1974 and married a young Hawaiian named Curt Sumida. She had another child, a boy named Kaena, and divorced again after five years.

In 1979 Bette moved to California, where her mother was then living, and began attending San Diego State University, where she eventually obtained a certificate in social work. She is proud of the fact that she has been drug-free and sober since 1983.

Jayne was by then in failing health. "She was a heavy smoker all her life, never gave it up, never wanted to give it up," Bette said. She died of emphysema at her home in Los Angeles in 1985. She was sixty-six.

Since 1985, having returned to Hawaii, Bette has been a substance abuse counselor at the Hawaiian State Prison for

Women at Kailua. She counsels with these women as one who has "been there," i.e., was addicted to drugs herself and has maintained her abstinence. "If I can do it, you can do it too," she tells the ladies at the prison.[3]

Nohea graduated from the University of Hawaii at Hilo in December 2001 with a degree in Hawaiian language and art, and has a six-year-old daughter. Nohea and her daughter are both fluent in Hawaiian.

LISA

Lisa, her younger sister, was the overachiever of the family, according to Bette. "She was younger and no one expected very much from her."

Lisa was just entering high school when the family broke up. "I loved my mother and I loved my father, and it was very, very difficult," she said, breaking into tears. "Most of the time I didn't know what was going on. It was pretty confusing."[4] She muddled through Midland High School, graduating in 1973. Her father decided that was a good time for her to begin learning about the family foundations, and she became a trustee of the Gerstacker Foundation at age eighteen.

She married an aspiring young Midland rock musician, but the marriage hit the rocks almost before it got out of the harbor. She picked up the pieces, returned to school, and graduated from Northwood Institute (now University) in Midland in 1979 with a degree in business and accounting. Apparently inheriting some of her father's extraordinary financial skills, she went on to become a CPA.

"My father said he never knew anyone who starved from giving away too much money," Lisa said. "Giving both time and money was in his soul and he encouraged it always—and we are focused on keeping that spirit alive."

She remarried—a musical instrument technician and judo champion named Sean Walsh—and they live in the mountains outside Boulder, Colorado, with their daughter, Katie. She is a vice president of both the Gerstacker and Pardee Foundations, and trustee of a variety of organizations, including Alma College in Michigan and the Pardee Home Foundation in Oakland, California.

TREE LOVER

From his boyhood on, Carl Gerstacker loved trees. Trees were his relaxation. He loved to walk among them and to take care of them. He could identify most of the native Michigan and Ohio trees by name and knew where they liked to grow, and what their habits were. He also knew quite a bit about their problems and their enemies.

Sandra Joys, his stepdaughter, told of thumbing through a book, the "Rocky Mountain Tree Identifier," that she picked up at his property in Colorado. He had penciled in his own hand-written notes in the margins, adding his own clues for identifying a particular tree to those of the experts.

113

The first piece of property he bought after he came back to Midland at the end of World War II was a tract of land at what is called "The Birches," on Lake Wixom about twenty miles northwest of Midland. Most of his neighbors at the place were friends from Midland—Charley Short, the proprietor of Nehil Lumber; Jim Bandeen, of Bandeen Chevrolet; Phil Rich, publisher of the *Midland Daily News;* Emerson (Bud) Price, a Dow attorney; Harold S. (Doc) Kendall, a Dow executive, and later his son Jim, an attorney. Wixom Lake offered tolerably good fishing and he taught his children and grandchildren about fishing there, and willingly cleaned and fried their fish.

The place at Wixom became his favorite retreat. In the summer of 1948 he and his good friend Dick Thrune, a Dow engineer, designed and built a small cabin on Gerstacker's property, a rustic shack in the woods that he enjoyed the rest of his days. After a few years he installed running water in it, followed by indoor plumbing, but it never housed a telephone, a television set, or a computer.

He liked to stroll among the trees—mostly birches, pines, cedar, and tamarack in this part of Michigan—and admire their strength and majesty. When Dutch elm disease invaded Michigan in the late 1950s and 1960s he was devastated by the damage it did to thousands and thousands of trees in the area. Midland's streets had long been planted with elms and almost all of them sickened and died and were replaced with other species, a sorrowful process that continued for a generation.

As he cruised the woods in the Midland area he saw more and more dead elm trees, and he heard the experts say that it was better to remove them, to stop the contagion from spreading. He bought one of the new chain saws that were coming on the market, and began a one-man crusade against the Dutch elm disease, cutting down dead or dying trees and chopping them up for firewood. Every year he delivered firewood to a wide circle of friends for their fireplaces.

It was already too late to save the American chestnut, another of his favorites, but he contributed funding for research on the problem through the Gerstacker Foundation.

Over time, as he acquired more property at various places in the world, he carried his chain saw with him and worked away at removing dead and unsightly trees. Eventually he kept a chain saw or two at each of his properties, and he spent large chunks of his spare time in Midland cleaning up the woodlands of the area. He had the Dow board of directors pass a resolution authorizing him "and helpers" to remove dead elms from the extensive properties owned by the

company in the Midland area. Occasionally a Dow security man would hear a chain saw operating on Dow property somewhere and would come charging through the woods intent on stopping the pilfering of lumber from the company, only to find the chairman of the board working away on a dead tree with a big smile on his face.

The height of his sylvan admiration was centered on the Sequoia redwoods, the world's largest and oldest trees, and for a long time he harbored the ambition to own his own grove of redwoods. But redwood trees were highly coveted and protected, and it was almost impossible to find a piece of redwood property for sale.

Then one day in 1972 his friend Al (Alfred T.) Look, who had become general manager of Dow's Western Division in California, called him in Midland. "I think I've got what you've been looking for," he told Gerstacker, "a grove of redwoods for sale. It's not a very big piece of land, only about thirty acres, but it's full of magnificent trees, and I think it's probably about as good as you can do if you really want to buy some redwoods."

"Act as my agent, Al, and buy it as quickly as you can," Gerstacker shot back. "Don't lose it—get it while it's on the market."

The day he bought the redwoods was one of the happiest days of his life. He loved the big trees there from the first moment he saw them. From then on he spent a few days every year, usually around Labor Day, working on his redwoods, tidying up the surroundings, constructing walking paths, removing stray brush. Each year he would invite a few close friends to spend those few days with him, helping with the work. The site was a few miles from Mendocino, the California art colony on the coast about 100 miles north of San Francisco. He and his guests stayed at the Little River Inn, a fine hostelry just a few miles down the road.

115

"I don't think Carl was ever as happy as he was working in those redwoods," Look said. "He was like a kid with a new toy. Taking care of them was his pride and joy."[5]

Heart of the Whirlwind

Gerstacker was still serving as chairman of the National Export Expansion Council when Richard Nixon ran for re-election in the fall of 1971. During that campaign the Economic Club of Detroit invited Nixon to spell out his economic policies in a visit to Detroit, and he accepted, asking that a panel of club members be selected to ask him questions about it. Gerstacker was immediately tapped to be one of the four questioners. At the time the nation was in the midst of a ninety-day wage and price freeze imposed by Nixon in an effort to stop runaway inflation.

116

Most of the questions asked by Gerstacker and his colleagues had to do with "Phase II"—i.e., what was to follow the ninety-day freeze, which was almost as unpopular as the war in Vietnam, then winding down. Some 3,000 demonstrators picketed Detroit's Cobo Hall, protesting both the freeze and the war, as the club members arrived for the president's appearance.

Nixon did not reveal very much about his post-freeze economic program at the session, saying only that it would be more selective, and that it would have teeth—but it was still the top news story of the day.

Gerstacker told the press that he liked the president's answers, that they made a lot of sense to him economically, and that he would continue to back the president's efforts to get the economy back on the track. "It is pretty exciting to be involved in this kind of event," he said. "It makes you feel like you're at the heart of the whirlwind."[6]

U-TURNS

One of the most remarkable features of Gerstacker's career was his expert, almost uncanny practice of the U-turn. Time and time again he started in one direction, and then effortlessly turned in the opposite direction and found himself heading in a direction diametrically opposed to the course he had initially pursued.

In October 1941 he joined the America Firsters, diehard isolationists who fought to keep the United States out of the war that was then looming. "We're making a terrible mistake if we get into this war," he wrote his parents, "and I mean to fight against our doing that as long as I can."[7] A few weeks later, after Pearl Harbor, he was one of the strongest proponents of the war that you could find.

When the environmental age dawned in 1962, Gerstacker viewed it initially as a direct attack upon the manufacture and use of chemicals and opposed it strongly. By 1966 he had performed a U-turn on the subject and had become one of the leading advocates of industrial responsibility in the field.

In 1954, when the Dow board of directors considered a proposal that it license the Ziegler process for making polyethylene and enter the polyethylene business, Gerstacker opposed the project violently. (Karl Ziegler, of the Max Planck Institute at Mulheim, Germany, was inventor of the leading process for making polyethylene plastic.) He contended that Dow was going into the product too late—Dow was actually the fourth of an eventual eight U.S. companies to license from Ziegler and enter the business—and that the company was likely to lose its shirt in such an enterprise. When he was outvoted and the project was approved, and the polyethylene venture became a big success, Gerstacker again did a U-turn and became one of the company's most ardent supporters of its polyethylene business.

But the most spectacular U-turn of his career was surely the reversal of his attitude toward the Japanese. In a few years he went from implacable enemy to warm friend of the Japanese and in the end, probably did more to encourage strong business ties between the United States and Japan than anyone else of his generation.

Freshly returned from the war, it will be remembered, he led the opposition to a proposed joint Dow-Japanese venture in 1951. In the succeeding years, however, he followed with great interest the development of the resultant company, Asahi-Dow Ltd., and took a leading part in the steady expansion of Dow's business in Japan.

He got along well with the Japanese from the start, became friends and golfing buddies with a variety of Japanese industrial leaders, and was frequently interviewed by the Japanese media when he was in that country. Indeed, over a period of time he became better known in Japan—more of a celebrity—than in the United States.

118

When Richard Nixon formed an Advisory Council on Japan–U.S. Economic Relations in early 1971 to advise his administration on economic policy in relation to Japan, Gerstacker was immediately named its vice chairman. He moved up to chairman in March 1973 (Najeeb Halaby of Pan American Airways was the first chairman). The council was composed of fifty top executives of American companies doing business with Japan, and it worked in concert with a Japanese counterpart, the Japan–U.S. Economic Council. Periodically the two groups organized U.S.–Japan Businessmen's Conferences, and Gerstacker became chairman of the U.S. delegation to these events. Henry Kissinger, when he was secretary of state, appointed Gerstacker to a three-year term as a member of the Joint Committee on U.S.–Japan Cultural and Educational Cooperation in February 1974. In 1976

Pres. Jimmy Carter appointed him a member of the Japan–U.S. Friendship Commission upon its formation.

All these connections gave him considerable prominence in Japan.

Toward the end of 1973 he learned that his friend Yoshizane Iwasa, chairman of the Fuji Bank, with whom he had had various business dealings, had recommended him to be the keynote speaker at the biggest upcoming Japanese economic gathering, the annual Symposium on International Economic and Business Cooperation in Tokyo. A formal invitation from Mitsuo Mutai, president of the *Yomiuri Shimbun,* followed shortly.[8] The *Yomiuri Shimbun,* with a daily circulation of 6.6 million, is one of Japan's largest and most influential dailies—it has an English-language sister paper, the *Daily Yomiuri,* which is more familiar to American visitors to Japan—and is the sponsor of this symposium with strong support from the Keidanren, the all-powerful Japanese Federation of Economic Organizations.

Gerstacker cancelled a scheduled January trip to Japan and accepted the Yomiuri invitation for April instead. Gerstacker had been headed to Japan because Dow Chemical common stock was being listed on the Tokyo Stock Exchange—the first foreign company so listed; because of his speaking engagement he arranged for Paul Oreffice, then Dow's chief financial officer, to head up the Dow delegation to the Stock Exchange celebration.[9]

The theme for the symposium that year was the world energy crisis, then at its peak, and Gerstacker was asked to give the Japanese his advice on how they ought to conduct themselves in view of that crisis. With Kogoro Uemura, president of the Keidanren, presiding, he launched into that subject, delivering his opening comments in Japanese and asking permission to speak as if he were, for a short time, a Japanese.

119

In this, his maiden effort at public speaking in Japanese, he even cracked a little joke in the language ("Already, several Yomiuri people have told me, 'Yes, we are 100 years old this year.' This is amazing. Not one of these persons looked to be anywhere near 100 years old").

"Some weeks ago I was having lunch in New York with two of the Arab oil leaders," he told them, "Minister of Petroleum Yamani of Saudi Arabia, Minister of Industry & Energy Abdessalem of Algeria, and I asked them to imagine for a moment that they were Japanese, and to tell me what they would do, if they were Japanese. This seemed to be a difficult question for them. Finally they said two things: first, they said, it should be understood that they liked the developed countries, such as Japan, and did not want to hurt their economies. And second, if the U.S. were able to become self-sufficient in energy and Japan were not, would this not be a U.S. problem? The United States, in other words, cannot be an island in an oil-short world."

Having received no answers to his question from the Arab leaders, he said, he asked himself the same question, and came up with seven basic suggestions as his prescription for Japanese action in the face of the energy crisis.

1. Conservation of Japan's oil and energy sources, in every way possible, seemed the most obvious answer to the problem.
2. Japan should "become as self-sufficient in energy as possible, as soon as possible," and to accomplish this Japan should "undertake a massive long-range research program, the greatest of its type in its history, to develop alternative energy sources for Japan."
3. Japanese industry must make major adjustments "to emphasize products that use low amounts of oil and energy in their manufacture, and conversely de-emphasize

products that use high amounts of oil and energy in their manufacture, such as electronics and automobiles. . . ."

4. Japanese foreign trade should adjust itself to the new reality of the energy crisis. "I would attempt to adjust our [Japanese] world trade in the sense that I would attempt to import more of those items that have a high energy content, and emphasize the export of items with a low energy content."

5. "I would urge upon my [Japanese] colleagues the necessity of accepting large new investments in Japan by foreigners."

6. "As a Japanese I would carefully study capital outflows from Japan. Most of our normal outflow must be devoted to buying oil and energy resources for Japan."

7. "And finally, I believe that as a corollary to all these efforts we should try, as Japanese, to develop and exert leadership in the energy field in the international arena. . . . The harmony of transactions between the oil-producing and oil-consuming nations and the maintenance of international order in this area have become matters of transcending importance."

In the final portion of this major address he resumed speaking in Japanese, and said that "the sun is the ultimate source of all our energy on this planet, that same sun that is displayed on the Japanese flag, the symbol of Japan. . . . It seems to me that in the energy crisis this symbolism takes on a new dimension of meaning. Japan is being challenged to produce another miracle—the energy miracle. And her flag clearly already says that she can do it. I believe every Japanese should see in his flag the encouragement and the inspiration to do this, and the confidence that it will be done."

And finally, he concluded, "let me express again my pleasure at the honor you have paid me today. Especially let me

121

thank you for the privilege of being, at least for this brief time, a Japanese."[10]

What his audience did not know, as they drowned him in applause, was that Gerstacker had been undergoing major dental work back in Midland at the time of this trip and that he had delivered the address with a mouthful of temporary teeth in preparation for the installation of permanent crowns and fixtures once he returned to Midland. He had told his dentist, Dr. Eldon Bailey, before leaving for Japan, "Eldon, I am going to Japan to address 500 of the top industrial leaders in the country, and if these temporaries come out while I'm in the act of giving my speech, I'm going to tell all those Japanese who my dentist is." He and Dr. Bailey both laughed, and the temporaries remained fixed until he got back to Midland.

In the end the Japanese did not follow his advice, but his counsel provided a basis for discussion of the nation's stance for several weeks afterward.

ESTHER

Back in Cleveland, Esther Schuette had been the fifth of seven children of the Little family. Her father, a canny old Scot, single-handedly ran the W. P. Little Used Machinery Co., which bought and sold old machinery in the thriving industrial metropolis on the lake. Some of the machines he bought he could never sell, and others he was able to sell for two or three times what he had paid for them. When times were good he made out quite well.[11]

She grew up to be a strikingly beautiful blond girl with blue eyes and followed her siblings to West Technical High School, where she graduated with honors—salutatorian of her class—and met the love of her life, William H. Schuette.

Bill, the school's star athlete—quarterback of the football team, stalwart of the baseball and basketball squads, all-city in football and basketball—was two grades ahead of her and was also salutatorian of his class. Upon graduation he went on to Cleveland's Case Institute of Technology to study chemical engineering. Esther graduated in 1932, in the depths of the Depression, and had no money to go to college. She was able to secure a scholarship, however, and went off to Hiram College, a small liberal arts school about forty miles from Cleveland. James A. Garfield, a former U.S. president, had once been president of the school.

She recalled that Bill would rush down to Hiram to see her, and could negotiate the distance between his door in Cleveland and hers in Hiram in forty minutes flat in his father's car. When she was a junior she had a severe accident. "Someone spilled sulfuric acid on the floor in Chem Lab and I came along and slipped on it and fell," she said. She suffered serious acid burns, especially on her knees and arms, and was hospitalized for months. She lost her chance to graduate with her class, and in the end took a crash course at a business college and got an office job, working in the Cleveland office of the *Saturday Evening Post*.

She and Bill were married in 1940, by which time he had earned a Ph.D., and Bill went on to a meteoric career with the Dow Chemical Company. By 1959 he was a member of its board of directors and had been selected to be the next president and chief executive of the company when, without warning, on 8 November of that year, he was struck down by a massive heart attack and died. Esther, then forty-five, was left with three growing children—Sandra, sixteen, Gretchen, thirteen, and William Duncan Schuette, who was only six.

The death was doubly tragic for her because at that time the company had no provisions to provide financial help in such a case. "The company did give me some kind of a

123

pension, which now you would laugh at if you heard how much it was," she said. "I don't think I would've gotten that if it hadn't been for Carl. I think he stepped in."

She went back to work, a three-day-a-week job in the Human Relations Development Department at Dow. "I was supposed to teach secretaries how they should treat their bosses, and bosses how they should treat their secretaries," she said. "I did that for two or three years. I don't think I was too good at it. I never had any training at all for it, except that I liked people and the girls. There was one period when the girls were supposed to criticize each other, and one little smart-aleck popped up and said, 'How about we criticize you?' I decided that was fair enough, and she said, 'Your hair is awful.' I thought, 'Boy, I've been a great success.' I kind of lost my enthusiasm for the job after that."

With three children in school—and her intention was that all three should complete college—she had major financial problems, and Carl Gerstacker become her financial adviser, dropping by from time to time to go over her finances with her. The Schuettes and Gerstackers had been social friends and had occasionally traveled to the Greenbrier together. (The Greenbrier, where Dow executives had their annual physical exams, is a popular resort at White Sulphur Springs, West Virginia.).

Ten years later, after his divorce, they began to see each other more often, and "it began to be serious," she said. One day he invited her over to his "bachelor pad" on Bayliss Street, and served hot dogs and braunschweiger and potato chips. "I thought that was the strangest menu for dinner that I ever heard of," she said, "but that was all he knew how to do. He had never learned to cook and never did learn to cook anything more complicated than that. There was no dessert."[12]

They soon became steady dates, a situation that lasted for almost five years. "His first marriage had been such a mess

that Carl was extremely reluctant to marry again," Paul Oreffice said. "He was just so afraid he'd make another mistake."

After a while she began to accompany him on his travels, and when this happened he moved up to the first class section of the airplane where she insisted on traveling, and rented two separate hotel rooms, on which she also insisted. "No hanky panky for me," she said.

At this time Carl went on a building binge, deciding first to build a house in the Caribbean on the Catherineberg, the tallest peak on St. John in the U.S. Virgin Islands. On one of their annual trips to St. John the "troika" had learned that the Rockefeller brothers were turning the bulk of the island over to the U.S. government as a national park and wanted to liquidate their holdings in the island entirely, except for Caneel Bay. Gerstacker, Branch, and Doan bought what the Rockefellers were disposing of and then split it up amongst themselves.

Gerstacker hired a local architect, Glenn Spear, and gave him free rein to design and build a rambling house on top of the mountain—"Carl just loved to look out from there over the Atlantic," Esther said. Spear would hire local building crews as he could and they would go up and work on the place up on the mountain. From there Carl could see for miles, across the ocean to Tortola and the British Virgin Islands. Almost everything had to be brought in from outside, and had to be shipped in on a vessel that was going to stop at the little port of Cruz Bay, the main settlement of the island. It took about three years to build it, and a couple more to furnish it. The design was basically Danish colonial (the U.S. Virgins having been acquired when Denmark sold them to the United States during WWI), with lots of archways to take advantage of the ocean breezes to keep it cool. "The house has more than 200 arches in it," Esther said. "I set out to

125

count them once, but I stopped after I got to 200." The water supply was perhaps the most severe problem of all—the island had no water system at all—and enormous catchment tanks had to be built that filled up with water in the brief rainy season. All the furniture and furnishings had to be brought in as well, and it took a long time to put it all together. Once Esther bought some chests for the place in Korea. "They got there about two years later. It was a big job furnishing the place because you couldn't really find furniture down there. You can now," she said.

Next, with Esther cheering him on, he tackled another out-of-the-way place, building a cottage on a property he had purchased on Spring Creek, a trout stream that rushes down from the Rocky Mountains near Gunnison, Colorado. He contracted with a local craftsman, Steve Cappellucci, to build the place. "By the time we had it built it turned out to be too small, so we built another cottage on the other side of the Creek, and of course then we had to build a bridge to connect the two," she said.

They were married on 8 March 1975, by their friend the Reverend William T. Elliott, rector of St. John's Episcopal Church in Midland. He had been a "bachelor" for six years, and she had been a widow for fifteen. The groom was fifty-nine, and the bride was sixty-one. They spent their honeymoon on the Catherineberg.

SUCCESSION

At about the time of Gerstacker's second marriage the troika, in its regular meetings as well as at special meetings, began discussing the problem of putting in place their successors. Gerstacker would be sixty and Ben Branch would reach sixty-two the following year. Many years earlier, Gerstacker had

instigated a plan for keeping the Dow leadership young. Essentially, the plan required members of the Dow board of directors to relinquish active executive posts at the age of sixty and to retire from the firm at sixty-five. The interim five-year (at a maximum) period, during which board membership continued, came to be called "deceleration." It is an institution peculiar to the Dow company. In the years since it has been installed, a majority of the affected Dow directors have found deceleration to be useful to the company and rewarding to the individual, but some have felt they were "cast aside" in their most productive years and that the period of deceleration was a waste of time and talent. The value of the deceleration period is the subject of a debate that has continued into the twenty-first century. In any event, there was no question that Gerstacker and Branch had to set an example for future generations by following the plan. Ted Doan, having retired as CEO at the age of forty-eight, had blazed the trail for them.

127

The trio considered a lengthy list of candidates to be the next CEO of Dow, but quickly narrowed the serious contenders down to two: Earle B. Barnes, president of Dow Chemical U.S.A., and Zoltan Merszei, president of Dow Chemical Europe. Barnes, a thirty-five-year veteran of the company, had broad experience in research and manufacturing, but none in other fields, notably finance and the foreign field. Merszei, in contrast, had spent his entire Dow career outside the United States, and had no experience at all in manufacturing or research. The shortcomings of each were the strong points of the other.[13]

Branch made an informal survey of the Dow board members and found that Barnes was clearly favored by the board, with Paul Oreffice, then the chief financial officer, the second choice, and Merszei third. Oreffice was seen as a potential CEO, but at forty-seven years old, too young. The question

rested there, with Barnes a unanimous choice, while Gerstacker, Doan, and Branch discussed the most tempting of their options—combining the talents and experience of Barnes and Merszei, somehow, at the top of the company. Eventually, and reluctantly, however, they discarded that idea when it became apparent that the two men would never be able to work in harmony together.

Once it became clear that some combination of the two principal candidates was only a dream, the choice, as they discussed it together, began slowly to shift to Merszei to head the company. Youth and charisma, in the end, carried the day, and in August 1975 the troika made its unanimous recommendations to the board of directors and they were adopted. Earle Barnes and Zoltan Merszei were both promoted to executive vice presidents of Dow at that meeting, and Merszei was directed to move to Midland. Clyde Boyd was appointed the new president of Dow Europe and Oreffice became Barnes's successor as president of Dow Chemical U.S.A. G. James (Jim) Williams, general manager of the Plastics Department, became the new chief financial officer.

The final act of this drama was reserved for the following spring at the annual shareholders meeting on 5 May 1976. At that meeting Gerstacker announced his own retirement as chairman, and told a packed house that he would be succeeded as chairman by Ben Branch, and that Zoltan Merszei was being tapped to be the new president and chief executive officer of the company.

"I have been planning for many years to retire at age sixty," Gerstacker said. "I will be sixty years old this year [his sixtieth birthday was 6 August, three months hence], and it is time to turn things over to others. After almost forty years it is easy to leave active work with a company when you have complete confidence, as I do, in the men who will be doing the work you have been doing."[14]

After he announced the changing of the guard, Gerstacker seized the opportunity to deliver his formal swan song to the company. During his many years as chairman of the board he had always, at the conclusion of the business session, introduced the chief executive officer of the company, who then presented his annual state-of-the-company address to the shareholders. This time Gerstacker chose to deliver the main address himself. He had been doing some heavy analysis, and had prepared a summary of the advances the Dow company had made in the previous quarter of a century—which just happened to coincide with his career as an officer of the company.

In what he called "A Look at the Record—Dow 1950–1975," he reviewed the firm's accomplishments with respect to each of its major constituencies.[15] The review was illustrated with charts and graphs thrown up on a giant screen. "Let's take a look at what great things we've accomplished during my incumbency," was the broad but not explicitly expressed burden of his message. He ticked off these accomplishments one by one:

> *Suppliers.* Gerstacker began by pointing out that Dow buys thousands of materials, supplies, and services from small, medium-sized, and large companies in many countries. "Our purchases amounted to $100 million in 1950 but by 1975 they had grown to almost $3.5 billion, or about $10 million per day every day. . . . We encourage our suppliers to be growing and profitable firms themselves and a good place for their employees to work. The money we spend with them provides jobs, investment capital, and profits for others, and multiplies itself many times over throughout the world's economies. In recent years we have been emphasizing purchases from vendors made

up of minority employees in the United States. In 1975 our dollar purchases from these firms was tripled, and the number of minority firms from whom we are buying increased about sevenfold over the previous year."

Customers. "We sold almost $4.9 billion worth of our products last year to hundreds of thousands of customers. That is 22 times the amount we sold in 1950, when our sales were $220 million. When I came to work in 1938 Dow had annual sales of $25 million and I thought it was a big company; now we sell that much in less than 48 hours. . . . Our prices have risen considerably in the past several years because of dramatic rises in all our costs, such as construction, labor, taxes, interest, raw materials, and especially oil, gas, and energy. But we are the victims rather than the cause of inflation, and we have partially sheltered our customers from the inflation in our costs. The average increase in the price of our products in the U.S. over this 25-year period has amounted to 2.5 percent per year. At the same time, the quality of the products we sell has risen significantly. How many other products or services can you think of that have increased in cost less than three percent per year over the last 25 years?"

Governments. "Last year we paid $475 million in income taxes to governments. This is 24 times what it was 25 years ago and that amount has been growing at a compound rate of 13.6 percent per year. In every country where we operate the government is really the largest stockholder in our company because in income taxes alone, government takes about one-half of our profits. And of course, we pay many other taxes in addition to income taxes–the property tax, Social Security tax, use tax, franchise tax, and intangible tax, to mention a few. . . ."

General Public. "By and large, Dow has no plants in large cities. Essentially our plants are located in small towns or in places where there was no town at all before Dow came–such places as Midland [Michigan], Freeport [Texas], Plaquemine

[Louisiana], Terneuzen [The Netherlands], Stade [Germany], and Guaruja [Brazil]. Dow plant locations are good places to live and work. Our employees and the company work hard to make them model cities. We now have plants in 30 countries outside the United States. . . . We have brought to these countries the advantages of modern technology, safe operations, and a clean environment, as well as highly paid employment opportunities."

Pollution Control. "In my opinion Dow is No. 1 in the world in both its attitude and its accomplishments in solving pollution problems. Our approach to this is simply not to create pollutants, whether they are incompletely used raw materials or waste end-products. In many cases this policy allows us to make a profit on our investment in the solution of pollution problems; it also puts the task into a positive framework in which, as we firmly believe, it is good business as well as good citizenship to reduce pollution."

Toxicology. "We have been a pioneering leader in toxicology testing to determine the safety of our products. When vinyl chloride was determined to be a problem, the world discovered that Dow Chemical had tried to convince the U.S. government and public of the danger of vinyl many years ago and had put safe practices in effect in our own plants even though we couldn't convince others of the problem. The same pattern is true for a number of other products. As a consequence we are widely recognized for our leadership in this field and we have had many compliments from the Environmental Protection Agency for this, and we have even had compliments from some of the most severe critics of industry."

Employees. Dow "currently has 53,100 employees worldwide, including 31,200 in the United States . . . this is almost four times the employee population we had 25 years ago; our employment has been growing at more than five percent per year. . . . Our total employment costs amounted to about $1

131

billion, an average of $18,500 per employee. Our average cost per employee is among the highest, and probably is the highest, in the chemical industry worldwide; and it is also among the highest for any company of any type, anywhere. . . . We believe Dow employees produce more sales and profits per person than the employees of any similar company. To put it another way, Dow Chemical employees are paid very well, and they deserve it."

Exports. "About 6,000 of our U.S. employees, or one out of every five, produce products that are sold outside the United States. Our exports have grown from $18 million in 1950 to $465 million last year. . . . Dow's exports not only are a major contribution to the U.S. balance of payments, but also create many jobs in the United States; and they bring vitally needed quality products at a fair price to the peoples of other nations."

Layoffs. "For more than 15 years, we have been trying to minimize the employee layoffs which occur in recessions. The recession now ending has been the most severe we have experienced since the great depression of the 1930s. Dow's U.S. production, for instance, had to be reduced by more than 25 percent at the low point. Most companies laid off substantial numbers of their employees, but Dow in the U.S. had a maximum layoff of 100 people, or less than one-half of one percent of our workforce. There were no layoffs in large plants such as Midland and Freeport. Isn't that extraordinary? Doesn't it make you proud? Think what such a performance would have done for the entire country."

Earnings. "Your company has certainly conducted itself as a good citizen during this recession, but let me quickly and clearly say that this was not accomplished at the expense of the shareholders. Our 10 percent increase in earnings per share last year was the best in the world for large companies in our industry. In my opinion the steady employment we have achieved in a very unsteady economic period has been a superb achievement."

Shareholders. Here's a "surprising and important fact about our employees: 44 percent of them in the United States are Dow shareholders, including 22 percent of our hourly workforce, 31 percent of non-exempt salaried personnel, and 68 percent of the exempt salaried force. Each member of our Board of Directors owns more than 18,000 shares, or more than $2 million worth of Dow stock. I point this out to illustrate the deep commitment that every one of them has to this company. What other company can equal such a record of involvement by its employees, at all levels, in the fortunes of the company?"

Research and Development. "Today, 5,200 of our Dow people work on R&D, more than four times as many R&D people as we had 25 years ago. . . . Our research expenditures have been growing at a rate of 13 percent per year, and last year we spent $167 million on R&D. . . . We have reached the point where we receive an average of one patent each day in the United States. . . . The great advances in art and science through the ages have come about because creative people were supported in these endeavors. Today, companies like Dow have to a large extent replaced the wealthy patrons, churches, or governments who supported such creativity in past generations. It is the efforts and ideas of our research employees that keep our processes updated and competitive and provide new and better products."

New Products. "In respect to new products we have the artificial kidney, Rifadin antibiotic for tuberculosis and other diseases, N-Serve for growing crops, a system to replace soybeans in producing paper (which could save enough soybeans each year to feed two million babies), and a method of getting more oil out of old oilwells that could add 35 billion barrels and double the production of oil from known wells in the United States. . . . Dow's research is very expensive and occupies the full time of one out of every 10 of our employees, but it does wonderful things for mankind and it is essential to our progress."

133

Equal Employment Opportunity. "As I've mentioned, Dow's plants are not located in the large cities where the primary problem of minority unemployment occurs; and yet we are working very hard to increase the opportunities at Dow for the minorities of the United States. The government has been monitoring the performance of companies on this problem in recent years. Our Federal government is so pleased with Dow's performance that they have allowed us to begin a two-year experiment in self-regulation. ERDA (Energy Research and Development Administration), to whom we are responsible for this phase of our activities, is working closely with us on this program. We are the first (and so far as I know the only) company that they have put on a basis of self-regulation."

Safety. "In 1975, for the first time, every geographical area of Dow finished the year with a rate of less than one disabling injury per million manhours worked. And in 1975 for the sixth consecutive year we experienced less than one disabling injury per million manhours, worldwide. We estimate that in the United States alone there are 224 Dow employees who are uninjured but who would have been injured if our record had been only as good as the U.S. chemical industry average—and the U.S. chemical industry has one of the best safety records of any industry. Isn't that great? I think we should all feel good about such an achievement, even though we must do our utmost to make our record even better."

Dividends. "Our cash dividends per share last year were $1.45, and this was more than eight times the cash dividend per share of 1950, adjusted for the intervening stock splits and stock dividends. We are the only American industrial company we can discover which has never reduced its cash dividend since we started to pay regular dividends in 1911. We have increased our dividend every year for the last 17 years, and very few companies can make that statement. . . . The total market value of Dow Chemical (that is, the number of common shares times

the market price per share) increased in the last five years from $2.2 billion to $8.4 billion. This $6.2 billion increase in market value was the largest for any American company, even though there are many companies larger than Dow in sales, and assets, and employees. Putting it another way, Dow has created more wealth for its stockholders in the last five years than any other American company."

At the conclusion of this "review of superior performance" he paused to salute the "quality" of Dow employees. "I believe Dow employees, from the newest to the oldest and at whatever level of job, are the best people at their jobs of anyone in the world," he proclaimed. "Nothing else could explain the record I have reported here today."

Although the Dow company is "traditionally a growth company," he said, "in the last ten years our growth has actually accelerated. All Dow employees are responsible for this, of course, not just one or two of them. However, we all know that the chief executive always gets the lion's share of the blame when things don't go well, and therefore he should also be entitled to a substantial share of the credit when things are going great. We have had two chief executive officers in the past ten years: Ted Doan and Ben Branch. If you like what has happened, you might tell them so."

Amidst thunderous applause he made his way back to his seat. He was now no longer the chairman of the board. That job was Ben Branch's. He was now entering that interim phase of life called "deceleration." He was now an elder statesman.

135

7

ELDER STATESMAN,
1976–81

1976   On 16 June the America-Japan Society and American Chamber of Commerce in Japan honor Gerstacker at a joint luncheon in Tokyo.

On 17 June is awarded the Order of Industrial Service Merit Silver Tower by the government of South Korea. The award is made in the prime minister's office in Seoul and recognizes his contributions to development of the petrochemical industry in Korea.

On 13 July announces his retirement as chairman of the Advisory Council on Japan–U.S. Economic Relations after serving in this post for three years.

1977   On 28 February, in Tokyo, Emperor Hirohito confers on him Second Order of the Rising Sun, one of the highest Japanese honors, in recognition of his contributions to improvement of U.S.-Japan economic relations. Meets with Japanese prime minister Takeo Fukuda and urges that Japanese industry expand its production plants in the United States. News reports list him prominently among those being considered as U.S. ambassador to Tokyo.

Serves as executive-in-residence at Albion College.

138

1978   The troika—Gerstacker, Branch, and Doan—returns temporarily to action as reports pile up that Merszei's performance as Dow CEO leaves much to be desired. Gerstacker plays a leading role in the "seven days in May" that result in Merszei's ouster. Paul Oreffice, for whom Gerstacker has been mentor, becomes the new CEO.

1979   Achieves a long-term goal as, for the first time, more than fifty percent of Dow sales come from outside the United States.

1980   The Dow Bank goes public in its fifteenth year, selling twenty-five percent of its shares on the Swiss open market. In the fifteen years since its establishment it has become the largest foreign-controlled bank in Switzerland and the eighth largest in that country.

THE PHASE OF HIS LIFE CALLED "DECELERATION" BEGAN with a series of highly satisfactory and eminently enjoyable events. A month after his retirement as chairman he left on a rambling trip to the Orient, beginning with a stop in Tokyo. There, on 16 June, the America–Japan Society and the American Chamber of Commerce in Japan joined hands to honor him at a luncheon the two groups organized at the Tokyo Hilton hotel, with 156 attending from the American and Japanese business and diplomatic sectors. This became the occasion for his farewell address to his Japanese friends, and he talked at some length about "some of the things I think I have learned" in his long association with Japanese business. "I'm more thoroughly convinced than ever that Japan and the United States are natural partners," he said, "and this fact needs to be brought home to the Japanese people and to the American people more frequently and more powerfully than has been the case to date. One of the more encouraging developments of recent years is the growth of formal organizations to actively cultivate and nurture this partnership. The first meeting of the Japan-United States Friendship Commission took place in January of this year, and this, I think, is one of the bright new things on the U.S.–Japan horizon, and I'm pleased to be a member of that commission."[1]

Then he and Esther flew off to Seoul, where he was honored by the government of South Korea the next day. There Dow was helping the Koreans build a world-scale petrochemical project at Yeochun (also called Yeo-Su), where Dow and the Korea Pacific Chemical Corporation (of which Dow owned fifty percent) planned to make chlorine, caustic soda, ethylene dichloride, vinyl chloride, and low density polyethylene, beginning in 1979. As one of the strongest backers of this project, Gerstacker was honored with the Order of Industrial Service Merit Silver Tower in recognition of his

139

contributions to development of the petrochemical industry in Korea. The award was presented by Prime Minister Choi Kyu-Hah at the prime minister's office in Seoul.

A month later, as he had informed the Japanese he intended to do, he retired as chairman of the Advisory Council on Japan–U.S. Economic Relations. He had served for three years.

It was not to be his last visit to Japan, however. A few months later he was called back to Tokyo to be awarded another high honor, the Second Order of the Rising Sun, conferred only at the express wish of the emperor and given in Japan only to cabinet members seventy years of age or older. In February 1977 he met with the Japanese prime minister, Takeo Fukuda, to receive the award, and as he usually did on such occasions he had some advice for the Japanese. He told Fukuda that the Japanese would be well advised to expand their production plants in the United States, especially for the production of automobiles, before public opinion in the United States forced them to do so. (In the following years the Japanese did expand their plants in the United States, but it is impossible to know how much of that can be attributed to Gerstacker's advice.)

The *Daily Yomiuri* and other Japanese publications more than once listed Gerstacker as a prominent contender to be the next ambassador to Tokyo. Those rumors were scotched when President Jimmy Carter paid off a political debt and named Leonard Woodcock, retiring president of the United Auto Workers, as his ambassador to the Japanese.

Gerstacker was also a member of the Science and Technology Advisory Group of the Republic of China (Taiwan), a small group that convened once or twice a year in Taipei to discuss questions posed by the government. The arrangement included first-class travel to Taiwan for the meetings for both Gerstacker and his wife, and for Esther this was a new world

opening up. She launched into a serious study of the Chinese language with her Midland friend, Jane Tou, in order to be able to participate in the numerous social events that accompanied the serious consideration of economic and scientific policy questions her husband was discussing with the Taiwanese.[2]

LEGIONNAIRES' DISEASE

In the early fall of 1974 he took Esther on his annual trip to the redwoods in California, but came down with what seemed at first to be a bad cold. It got rapidly worse, and he seemed to be producing heavy phlegm in his lungs faster than he could get rid of it. On the advice of their friends at the Little River Inn they consulted a young doctor at Ft. Bragg, a dozen miles north, who immediately diagnosed it as Legionnaires' Disease and warned Gerstacker he was in danger of his life. Over the next few weeks they battled the malady together. Every day the young doctor, who had made a study of respiratory ailments, almost literally beat the accumulating phlegm out of Gerstacker's lungs. The next day he would have to do it over again. "That man saved my life," Gerstacker said later. "I was so lucky to stumble on a doctor who knew respiratory problems and knew exactly what to do."

141

That was also the occasion when he quit smoking cigarettes. The doctors told him quite bluntly that if he valued his health at all he had to quit, and he did. He had been smoking almost forty years—Salem mentholated cigarettes for most of those years, at a rate of about two packs a day—and he told friends that quitting was one of the most difficult things he had ever had to do. But he did it. Esther was happy about it for she had been badgering him to quit for years.

MASTERS AND JOHNSON

For a twenty-year period beginning in about 1965, Masters and Johnson were the most widely acclaimed and wildly successful sex experts in the United States and the world. They were at the cutting edge of the revolutionary change that was occurring at that time in American attitudes toward sex. They were the experts on the subject. They operated out of an organization called the Reproductive Biology Research Foundation (RBRF) in St. Louis, Missouri, where they conducted meticulous, academically impeccable research on sexual functioning and problems and regularly published their findings, which almost always became runaway bestsellers as soon as they appeared.

When the courtly, seemingly aloof Dr. William H. Masters told Gerstacker he would like to talk to him "about a professional matter," Gerstacker was immediately intrigued, but he told Masters, "I don't know how I can help you—I don't know anything at all about your business." Masters said they needed professional oversight to keep their finances straight, and that Gerstacker had been recommended to him. "I'm told you're the best financial whiz there is, and that you're honest, and that you can be painfully honest if it's needed," Masters told him. "Will you join our board of directors, and keep an eagle eye on our finances? We badly need your kind of help."

In the years that followed, Gerstacker often carried on his travels a volume or two of the esoteric sexual studies that were to be discussed at the next board meeting of the RBRF, and used them as bedtime reading instead of the Louis Lamour westerns that he usually favored. "Most of these academic sex studies are tough reading," he said at the time. "It was difficult for me to believe it, but sex can actually be made to be boring."

He became a warm friend of both Masters and of Dr.

142

Virginia Johnson, his research associate who had become Mrs. Masters, and his association with them became well known in business circles. Indeed, Gerstacker discovered that he was actually envied by a large portion of the business people he knew. His directorship of Masters and Johnson was one of the most prestigious he could have had. At a gathering of chemical industry moguls Perry Wilson, board chairman of Union Carbide Corporation, told Gerstacker he would trade any three of his own board memberships for Gerstacker's board membership with Masters and Johnson. The remark got a good laugh, but there was more than a grain of truth in it.

On one occasion Masters and Johnson came to Midland to visit the Gerstackers and agreed to speak informally to a gathering of friends in the Gerstacker living room after dinner. A question-and-answer session was to follow their remarks, and Carl volunteered to ask the first question to get it started. Masters and Johnson delivered two charming talks concerning their activities and asked if there were any questions. Carl's hand went up in the front row. "Dr. Masters," he said, "or maybe this is for Dr. Johnson. Can you tell me what your research shows, and what your recommendations are, for people suffering from premature ejaculation?"

Esther, sitting next to him, was visibly embarrassed. "Carl," she said, "what an awful thing to ask."

For Masters and Johnson, however, it was just a routine question.

143

ALBION

His life was full of contradictions, and it was typical of him that the institution of higher learning that came to be closest to his heart would also be one to which he owed no visible debt of love or loyalty.

In the fall of 1960, a few weeks after he had become chairman of the Dow board, he received a call from Dr. Louis W. Norris, president of Albion College, a small liberal arts school in southern Michigan with a Methodist church background and tradition. Dr. Norris told him that Mark Putnam had been a trustee of the college for years and that they were sorry to lose him (Putnam had died in the first week of November), but he would now like to ask Gerstacker to join the board of trustees to replace Dr. Putnam. "We'd like to maintain the tie with Midland and with Dow Chemical," Dr. Norris said.

"I had heard that it was, if not the best, just about the best small liberal arts school around," Gerstacker told a reporter later. "Plus, the University of Michigan [his alma mater] didn't want me as a trustee."[3]

He joined the Albion board of trustees without ever having set foot on the campus, and as a later president of the school said, "became one of the guiding lights of Albion for the next 30 years."[4]

He began by familiarizing himself with Albion's financial situation as a member of the board's finance committee. In 1965 he became vice chairman of the board for finance and business affairs, and served in that position the next twelve years. He then became chairman of the board in 1977 and served in that position for six. He served as a trustee for twenty-eight years in all, until 1988. He once said he had only two conditions for his service to Albion—first, that the college pursue excellence in all its endeavors, and, second, that he himself could make a difference.

Along the way he funded construction of a building devoted to the college's international program, the Gerstacker International House. Albion became one of the top recipients of grants from the Gerstacker Foundation. When he retired from the Dow Chemical board in 1981, his fellow directors memorialized the event by establishing the Carl

A. Gerstacker Scholarship Fund at Albion with a gift of $125,000, and to be a Gerstacker Scholar at Albion soon became a mark of distinction.

In 1977, the same year he became the Albion board chairman, Gerstacker also became its first Distinguished Visiting Professor of Economics and Business, and spent the week of 28 March that spring teaching classes on the campus, which he enjoyed fully. In the fall of 1977 he filled that role again, and he did it a third time in April of 1989. In 1972 the college bestowed on him an honorary Ph.D. (his second), and in 1983 he was the commencement speaker and received the college's Distinguished Service Award.

Throughout his service to the school he supported a program called the Liberal Arts Program in Professional Management, basically designed to bridge the gap between a liberal arts education and a business career, and participated regularly in its activities. The mission of this program was "to turn out graduates who can not only do something exceptionally well but also know what is most worth doing." He headed up a successful $1.5 million drive to fund this program.

His contributions to the college were so many and so enduring that when he announced in early 1988 that he was leaving the Albion board after twenty-eight years it came as something of a shock. Feeling that they ought to do "something extra special" to honor him, the trustees and college settled upon a full day of events on the campus dedicated to Carl A. Gerstacker. The agenda began with an open house and continued with a panel discussion by Gerstacker Scholars, presentations by students in the Program in Professional Management, and a symposium on "American Business: What It Takes to Be Competitive."

Six of the nation's top corporate leaders were assembled to discuss this topic, all of them close friends of Gerstacker:

145

Joseph E. Antonini, chairman and CEO of K-Mart Corporation (Gerstacker had been chairman of the K-Mart board committee that selected Antonini to be the CEO of K-Mart); John H. Bryan, Jr., chairman and CEO of Sara Lee Corporation (Gerstacker had been a member of the Sara Lee board for many years); John S. (Jack) Ludington, chairman and CEO of Dow Corning Corporation (Gerstacker had been chairman of the executive committee at Dow Corning and a long-time board member); Dr. Paul W. McCracken, Edmund Ezra Day Professor of Business Administration at the University of Michigan and chairman of the President's Council of Economic Advisers under President Nixon (Gerstacker had gotten acquainted with McCracken in Washington and later recruited him to the Dow Chemical board of directors); Paul F. Oreffice, who was then the Dow board chairman (for whom, as mentioned above, Gerstacker had been mentor); and Gerstacker himself.

146

Each of the six had different prescriptions for the nation's economic ills, and they thoroughly enjoyed arguing about it. Gerstacker stole the show when the discussion touched on the then–current attempts to keep South Korea, Taiwan, and Japan within the capitalistic orbit. "Is anyone in Michigan afraid of the Russian automobile makers?" Gerstacker asked. "Let 'em go communist!"

At the end of the day they all gathered for a gala dinner at which the main business was the renaming of the Program in Professional Management as the Carl A. Gerstacker Liberal Arts Program in Professional Management. Congressman Bill Schuette, Gerstacker's stepson, read a letter congratulating Gerstacker on receiving this honor, signed by Ronald Reagan. Willie Davis, a former Green Bay Packer and member of the National Football League Hall of Fame, was a special speaker at the program. He had become a director of Dow Chemical several years before.

"Carl Gerstacker is one of the finest human beings I know," Davis said. "The guy just leaves an impression on me as a wonderful human being." At the end of the evening there was a standing ovation for Gerstacker which went on for several minutes. Gerstacker finally took out a small whistle he carried and blew a halt to the ovation with it. "It was very embarrassing," he said.

He was visibly moved by the whole affair. "I've never been so happy in my whole life," he told the assemblage. "I have never had so many friends that I love so much all in one room at one time. Thank you, thank you, thank you, all you wonderful people."

THE SEVEN DAYS IN MAY

By the mid-1970s Dow Chemical was the world's most profitable chemical company, and profit was the yardstick by which the Dow leadership measured success. Sales volume was secondary for Dow—earnings, or profit, whichever you called it, was the bottom line. Beginning in 1974 Dow's earnings surpassed even those of Du Pont, which had been the world leader in chemicals for many years, and Dow continued to lead the world chemical industry in 1975, 1976, and 1977. Those were glory years for Dow.

The troika which had led Dow to these heights—Doan, Branch, and Gerstacker—turned the reins over to its successor, Zoltan Merszei, in 1976, in the midst of this success. Although Merszei became president and CEO, the troika did not completely relinquish authority, as Gerstacker remained chairman of the Finance Committee, Doan was still a board member, and Branch, Zoltan's mentor, was the board chairman. Still, it was Zoltan's show, and with his cavalier style it was, almost from the start, a one-man show. Aside from the

147

monthly meetings of the board of directors the troika interfered very little in his management of the firm.

Merszei had won his way to the top with sustained brilliance as the head of Dow Europe, where he had built an organization virtually from scratch that had made Dow the leading U.S. chemical firm on the continent. The troika was hopeful that he could carry this same magic touch to the worldwide company, and they had turned him loose to do so, if he could.

During the first year or so of Merszei's leadership the prosperity continued in full bloom. Profits continued to be the best in the business. In the third year of his stewardship, however, they started to became uneasy for they discovered that a revolt was brewing beneath the surface. Earle Barnes, executive vice president, and Paul Oreffice, president of Dow USA, were among those letting it be known that they were ready to leave the company. It was becoming increasingly clear that the autocratic managerial methods that had succeeded so brilliantly in Europe were not proving to be applicable to the corporation as a whole—indeed, were threatening to cause it harm.[5] Schooled to make, and to enjoy making, their own decisions, Dow employees in the United States found themselves expected to take orders, not give them, and they did not like it. Without realizing it, Merszei was losing his troops.

Eventually the complaints reached such a level of volume and intensity that the troika reunited to discuss the situation and possible responses to it. Looking at it closely, they saw much cause for alarm, and soon agreed that immediate changes were in order. They also decided the first step was to talk to Zoltan about it, since he did not seem to be aware of it.

Gerstacker called Merszei in the next day and told him an open revolt was fomenting in the company, and that he and

Ben and Ted had discussed it and had concluded that the company "should have a new CEO within the next few months."

Merszei exploded in protest. "How can you do this to me?" he asked. "Why didn't anyone tell me I was doing something wrong, if I was? Why aren't you supporting me, as you should, instead of attacking me?"

He asked for an immediate meeting with all three members of the troika, which was arranged for the same evening, and the discussion went on late into the night. Merszei said that as it happened, a survey of Dow employee morale worldwide was being undertaken and that if anything were wrong it would show up there, and proposed that any further action be delayed pending the outcome of the survey. "How long will that take?" they asked. "Five months," Merszei said. "We can't wait that long," Branch said, and the others agreed.

At the board of directors meeting a few days later it was decided that a survey would indeed be made, but that it would be restricted to the fourteen board members other than the troika and Merszei (there was a total of eighteen board members). The survey would be made by two of the board members, Herb Lyon and Julius Johnson, who were scheduled for deceleration, each one to interview six members plus himself. The board also agreed to meet again on 28 April, before the annual meeting of shareholders, which was scheduled for 3 May, to consider the matter again. Those few days (six days, actually, and only three of them in May) became known in Dow lore as "the seven days in May."

Merszei lived across the street from Gerstacker on Valley Drive in Midland at the time, and most of the action of "the seven days," packed into the weekend of Friday, 28 April, to Sunday, 30 April, took place in the Gerstacker house and the Merszei house across the street from it. Directors alone and in groups drifted from one house to the other and one

149

discussion to another and then back to the other, for most of the weekend, as the neighbors curiously looked on.

The formal board meeting that followed on Monday morning, 1 May, was quite brief. Herb Lyon, speaking for himself and Julius Johnson, reported that the poll of the directors undertaken at the direction of the board showed that a majority favored the elevation of Zoltan Merszei to chairman of the board, succeeding Ben Branch (Branch's retirement having been tendered). A majority of the directors also supported the election of Paul F. Oreffice as new president and chief executive officer of the company. Merszei, standing, said, "I don't suppose I should stay for the vote," and left the room.

The formal vote on these changes was put off until the customary "organization meeting" of the board following the annual meeting of stockholders two days later, but the decisions already had been made on the first day of May. Merszei was out; Oreffice was in.

The matter of his "elevation" to the chairmanship was understood by the board members who voted for it as an alternative and gentlemanly way of avoiding the nasty business of firing Merszei outright. The chairmanship was to be a temporary platform while he searched for a position elsewhere—outside of Dow—and it was intended only to last for a few months at most. Branch and Gerstacker tried separately to explain this to him, but Zoltan could not bring himself to believe they were serious about it.

Several months went by and Merszei gave no indication of looking elsewhere for a new position. He was happy as the board chairman of Dow, and kept asking Gerstacker for added responsibilities. He wanted to be more involved in the company, and wanted to earn more than $250,000 a year, he told him.

Gerstacker said he thought a better idea would be for

Zoltan to take early retirement from Dow, or undertake a search for a top job at another company through some "head-hunting" firm. Merszei said he did not want to leave Dow, that he had spent thirty years there and had done a great job for the company, and that it could all be worked out if Gerstacker "forced" it to work.

"I can't make it work, Zoltan," Gerstacker said. He told him the kind of thing that was happening to him had happened many times to others. "Look at Lee Iacocca," he said, "he was fired at Ford and became a hero at Chrysler."

By 1 January of 1979 Gerstacker, Doan, and Oreffice were convinced that Merszei had no intention of leaving Dow unless he were forced to, and that they had to take action. On 9 January the three of them met with Merszei and Oreffice handed Merszei a letter he had prepared offering him the options of resigning, retiring, or being fired, and giving him until the 8 February meeting of the board of directors to decide which of these options he preferred. Merszei asked for time to think about it. No, they said, we've been telling you this for months; we mean "immediately." Gerstacker pointed out to him that if he did not retire or quit he would be fired, and being fired was the worst possible outcome for Zoltan. Merszei said he would try to meet the 8 February deadline. "Trying isn't good enough," Oreffice said. "That is the deadline."

151

Five days later Merszei met with Herb Lyon, the administrative vice president, for a discussion of separation details. On 8 February he handed in his resignation.

Two months later, on 17 April, Armand Hammer, chairman of Occidental Petroleum Company (known on the street as "Oxy Pete"), called a press conference to announce the appointment of Zoltan Merszei as vice chairman of that company, a newly created position. "When I look at him, I see a lot of myself in my younger days," Hammer said of Merszei. A

few months later he promoted Merszei to president and chief operating officer of the firm.[6]

BIG-TIME BANKING

When Gerstacker and the Dow Chemical Company bought forty percent of a venerable old bank in Amsterdam in 1963, it was somewhat of a surprise to the banking world but certainly understandable. After all, Dow was now dealing in dozens of currencies daily in its European business, and if it wanted to spend Greek drachmas in Italy, or Dutch guilders in France, it had to pay a commission fee, and the full fee at that, to translate drachmas into lira or guilders into francs. Currency translation quickly became a big expense item on the Dow balance sheet.

152

"Why should we pay all that money just to move from one currency to another?" Gerstacker wondered. "There must be a better way to do it." He turned the task of finding a bank to manage this problem for Dow over to John Van Stirum, an American of Dutch descent who spoke flawless Dutch and was familiar with the European business scene. Van Stirum recommended Bankierskantoor Mendes Gans, (BMG), "a small Dutch bank doing a big business" in Amsterdam. Eighty percent of BMG was owned by Philips N.V., the giant Dutch conglomerate headquartered at Eindhoven, which had much the same kind of exchange problem. Dow eventually bought half the Philips holding.

"The Mendes Gans Bank sits on the Herrengracht Canal, the most distinguished address in Amsterdam," said Bob Bennett (a son of E. W.), who had succeeded Gerstacker as company treasurer. "It has been declared an historical site. The president, Maut Ligtenstein, sits in an enormous office and he cannot touch the walls, the ceilings, or anything else.

Those rooms cannot be touched. They were the homes of Amsterdam's burgermeisters and now they are historical sites. Upstairs, however, was modern and reasonable. They moved the computers into another building. Forming a relationship with that bank was a very sharp move."[7]

BMG, Bennett explained, became Dow's financial turntable. "We could put all of the company's deutschmarks, kroner, and whatever other currencies into the Mendes Gans Bank, and they spewed it out in whatever quantity to suit whatever needs and times. It's a very efficient operation."

While BMG solved one of the company's major financial problems it didn't solve all of them. In 1964 Gerstacker saw signals that Washington was contemplating an embargo on U.S. investment abroad. Pres. Lyndon B. Johnson was conducting a campaign to "keep American dollars at home." Such a program would be catastrophic for Dow, Gerstacker recognized, with the company in the midst of building major facilities abroad, particularly at Terneuzen, the Netherlands, its largest European manufacturing site. An embargo would halt the company's expansion program in jig time, and leave it with half-built plants on its hands. Gerstacker reasoned that Dow should move some money abroad immediately, to draw on if the embargo were put into place.

153

He called in Bennett and Van Stirum, who had become assistant treasurer, and told them he wanted them to go to Europe. Their task was to look for a home for $50 million, which was to be Dow's hedge against the possibility of an embargo on U.S. investment abroad, which if imposed might last for years. He wanted them to find a place that would be safe, and that would pay a decent rate of interest. Heading immediately for Europe, Bennett and Van Stirum spent a week talking to Dutch bankers whom Van Stirum knew, proposing that they take Dow's $50 million and loan it out to very safe borrowers. Bennett said that the Dutch didn't want to do

this and they were told, "You ought to go someplace else." They headed for Switzerland and began talks with various Swiss bankers, but none of their suggestions seemed to be very satisfactory either. "Somewhere along the line, John Van Stirum came up with the idea of a Dow bank," Bennett said. When they got back to the United States they outlined this idea to Gerstacker, and "Carl, before Van Stirum could finish, declared, 'We can do this. They'll never let us have a bank, so we'll call it something else.' Van Stirum agreed, 'Gee, that's a good idea.' . . . We started out with something else and ended up with the Dow Bank about a year later."

The Dow Banking Corporation was chartered in May of 1965 in Zurich, and was an immediate success. "It worked very well, and we made money on it," Bennett said. "We made money on the $50 million that we put into it, and we made money, much later, selling the bank. Everybody loved the idea of having a bank. Zoltan Merszei liked the bank. Paul Oreffice liked the bank. Ben Branch liked the bank."

Bennett became the first chairman and Van Stirum the first manager. "I always loved to say I was chairman of a Swiss bank," Bennett said.

Gerstacker issued a public disclaimer when the Dow Bank was announced. "Let me stress," he said, "that Dow is in the chemical business; we have no desire to compete with bankers. Basically, our 1963 venture into Mendes Gans, Amsterdam, has made us more efficient in the European money market. Our 1965 entry into banking in Switzerland increases our capability in the European capital market. In both cases we obtained greater efficiency, lower costs and more know-how in an essential basic raw material of our company—money. We try to do this in every department of Dow and the treasurer's department is no exception."[8]

Ed Fassler, the first full-time employee of the Dow Bank and later its long-time general manager, said they called it

"backward integration." "The idea for the establishment of Dow Bank actually was that more and more American companies were looking to Europe to expand their business activities. Dow Chemical had a lot of customers but also a lot of competition: Bayer, Badische, ICI and so on. We approached Dow's customers, saying: 'We offer you banking services. You need credit, we look at it, we give it to you. You need transfers, you need foreign exchange, you need letters of credit. We are ready to be your banker.'"[9]

While the bank began with the aim of providing capital support for Dow's expansion in Europe, it went on from there and eventually became a bank specializing in medium-term Euro financing. "We were a wholesale bank, a merchant bank," Fassler said. "We refinanced our asset business by going to the Euromarket and establishing bank lines with many major banks in Switzerland, in Japan, in Germany, in New York, on the West Coast, and so on. That's how we financed our business. We bought our funds."

The old, established Swiss banks were at first amazed to find this brash American intruder in their ranks, but quickly decided to do business with them. "We came in with a hundred million Swiss francs capital, which was enormous at that time," Fassler said. "Van Stirum and I went together to see Alfred Schafer of Union Bank of Switzerland, who was the number one banker in Switzerland at that time. We did the same at Credit Suisse and at Swiss Bank Corporation, the number two and three banks. We told them we planned to open a bank. They were the big three, and still are today in Switzerland. They all said the same thing: 'You don't need a bank. We do everything for you. Why do you want to go to the trouble of establishing a bank and pay the taxes and hire people and take all the risks?' We did it anyhow. But the Swiss are businessmen and they know the old rule, if you cannot beat them, join them. We gave our Swiss franc bond issues to the

Swiss banks. They gave us lines, all three of them. They did business with us as with every other bank. No problem."

Much of the phenomenal success of the Dow Bank was ascribed to its flexibility, its creativeness, and a certain spirit of adventure, Fassler said. He remembered an early deal by the bank, in 1967, a so-called private placement for the government of Austria, twenty million Swiss francs at a fixed interest rate for five years. "Today, looking back, it is a ridiculously low amount," Fassler said, "but at that time it was real money. I was in Vienna when we signed the contract with the government, and during lunch I asked the treasurer of Austria, 'Why did you come to the Dow Bank? We are unknown. We are only two years old. Your country has been dealing with the Big Three Swiss banks for the last 100 years, through good and bad times.' And he said, 'Well, we did go to the other banks, but they said we don't have five-year money. And then you came and said, 'What do you need, 20 million? These are our conditions. Take it or leave it.' We took it.'"

By 1980, only fifteen years after its founding, the Dow Bank was the largest foreign-owned bank in Switzerland (of forty-six) and the eighth largest bank in all in that banking country, with more than two billion Swiss francs in assets. By then the world banking picture was changing rapidly, however, and Gerstacker decided it was time to take the bank public. It turned out to be not too difficult. It sold twenty-five percent of its shares on the open market in Switzerland. Fuji Bank of Japan purchased ten percent of the shares itself. The Dow Bank had begun some time before to attract imitators, and the field was getting crowded.

It turned out to be the beginning of the end. From that point on, as a public bank, the Dow Bank was either a competitor among the world's major banks, or it was not in the game. Its niche was disappearing. And Gerstacker remembered

what he had said in 1965—that Dow was in the chemical business, not out to compete with bankers. From there it was easy to reach the decision that the Dow Bank had served its purpose for the Dow Chemical Company and was no longer a valid activity.

In September 1986 the Dow Bank finalized its takeover by the Royal Trust Bank of Canada, one of the oldest and largest of the Canadian banks. It then became, and remains, the Royal Trust Bank (Switzerland).[10]

Although he never served on the board of the Dow Bank, throughout its history Gerstacker was viewed as the power behind the throne, as he undoubtedly was. Walter B. Wriston, president of New York's National City Bank, on whose board Gerstacker did serve, once observed in introducing Gerstacker that "he took more money away from banks than Jesse James did."

There was a lot of truth to that.

157

BOARD MEMBER

Gerstacker's fame in the industrial world was based largely on his service on the boards of directors of leading American firms. He was renowned for his ability to ask a few brief questions during a board meeting that would get to the heart of a proposal and skewer its weaknesses.

Six years after Gerstacker's death, John Bryan, chairman of Sara Lee Corporation, was asked what made a good board member, and he cited Gerstacker. "Dow Chemical had a great safety record, and Carl decided that as long as Sara Lee's safety record wasn't as good as Dow's, he was going to beat the hell out of us. He very politely and nicely did that for two or three years . . . Carl was a marvelous example of a board director who identified an important way in which he could

contribute and didn't wait until there was a crisis that demanded his expertise. He made an enormous difference to Sara Lee."[11]

Gerstacker was, "without question, a Dow icon," said Robert M. Keil, executive vice president and chief financial officer of Dow in the Oreffice era, and "an extraordinary financial presence." Keil recalled an incident that occurred after Gerstacker had retired. Dow was considering the purchase of another company, and asked him to attend a small meeting at which this was discussed. "He said, 'if you do that, you had better be prepared for this, and this is the way the deal is going to ultimately happen.' He projected what would occur. He projected the price for which the company was going to sell, and he missed it by two percent, which really impressed me."

"I've never seen Carl as a dramatic leader," said Keil. "I've seen him more as the knowledgeable, thoughtful, analytical person."[12]

Long after he had retired, Gerstacker phoned Keil one day and said he was calling as a stockholder, not as a former chairman. He said he had just read the company's annual report and noted that the president's message featured "a great cost savings program" that Dow was instituting. "How can you do that and then turn around and spend $1.39 per copy to deliver the report in an envelope first class?" Gerstacker wanted to know. "I have checked with the post office and about 20 cents would have done the job without the envelope." Keil responded, "Mea maxima culpa," and promised to look into it instantly. He asked his staff to report to Gerstacker, suggesting they do so by "a handwritten note on used scratch paper, delivered by the cheapest means available."[13]

8

PHILANTHROPIST, 1981–87

1981 Serves as chairman of 1981 Community Fund Drive in Midland.

On 13 August retires from Dow board of directors and related functions, one week past sixty-fifth birthday. Board names him "Director Emeritus" in recognition of "extraordinary and unparalleled contributions to the company over an extended period of time"—the only person ever so honored.

Is now a director of Consolidated Foods Corporation (predecessor of Sara Lee), K-Mart Corporation, Spence Engineering Company, National City Corporation, Chemical Financial Corporation and Chemical Bank & Trust Company, and a trustee of the Michigan Molecular Institute and of Masters and Johnson Institute. Is chairman of trustees of Albion (Michigan) College and a member of the Science and Technology Advisory Group of the Republic of China (Taiwan) and of the advisory board of New Perspective Fund, Inc., Los Angeles.

Is both an elder of Memorial Presbyterian Church, Midland, and a vestryman of St. John's Episcopal Church, Midland.

160

1983 Steps down as board chairman of Albion College.

1984 As anonymous donor, inaugurates program to "help those who really need it" in columns of *Midland Daily News* under the name of "Barley MacTavish, problem solver."

Bill Schuette, stepson, runs for Congress against an entrenched incumbent, Don Albosta. In midsummer, with campaign in disarray, Gerstacker steps in and becomes campaign manager and reorganizes campaign. Schuette wins, after a recount, by 1,314 votes. "I couldn't have won without him," Schuette says.

1985 City of Midland establishes a Downtown Development Authority with Gerstacker as a charter member, and he becomes actively involved in renovation of downtown Midland.

1986   Is named to the Garfield Society, the highest honor bestowed by Hiram College, Ohio.

On 12–13 September a flood invades Midland and the Gerstacker home. The Gerstackers, returning home from Taiwan at midnight, are unaware of the flood warnings and go straight to bed. They are awakened at 3 a.m. and find water already ankle-deep in their bedroom. Some hours later they evacuate the house, she by canoe and he by wading and swimming, escorting their two dogs on leash. They move to a small house at 1310 Michigan Street in Midland while their house and furniture are redone, moving back into their own home in March 1987.

1987   Serves on a committee to select a new city hall site for Midland.

On 27 April receives "Book of Golden Deeds Award" from the Midland Exchange Club.

Assists with efforts to establish a United Way organization in Gladwin, Midland's neighboring county to the north.

CONQUERING CANCER

He began a long career in philanthropy in 1944 with $1 million in Dow stock and a directive from his Aunt Elsa.

Uncle Jim Pardee—his "Unkie"—had died in January 1944, suffering from cancer the last few years of his life. His "Auntie" died the following October, also from cancer, having made out her will in August setting aside $1 million in Dow Chemical common stock for the purpose of solving the cancer problem—"for the care and cure of cancer," she stipulated. Carl and his sister Elsa were named the two trustees of the fund.

"Elsa and I felt that we had an awesome responsibility," he said later. "We had little knowledge of cancer or of the management of trusts or foundations. A number of people offered advice and we discussed whether to give the entire million dollars to one hospital or to the laboratory of a university, or to build a research laboratory, or give the money to a larger group like the American Cancer Society, or do it ourselves. We decided to try to do it ourselves by forming an organization that would promote the control and cure of cancer. Consequently, the two trustees formed the Elsa U. Pardee Foundation on 22 December 1944, with Eda U. Gerstacker, my mother, as president; my sister, Elsa G. Allen, vice president; Rollin M. Gerstacker, my father, as vice president; William W. Allen, Elsa's husband, as secretary; and myself, as treasurer." [1] (Rollin Gerstacker died of a heart attack only three months later.)

His nomination of himself as treasurer set a pattern for his philanthropic activities for the next fifty years—he was never the "front man" (i.e., chairman or president) of any of the foundations with which he was involved, and yet he was clearly the controlling factor in them most of the time. He was treasurer of the Pardee Foundation until his death, was

treasurer of the Gerstacker Foundation as well, and always had a good deal more influence than the job implied.

In 1945, its first year of operation, the Pardee Foundation gave a total of $24,000 to three institutions—$6,000 to Sloan-Kettering Memorial Hospital in New York, $8,000 to the University of Minnesota, and $10,000 to the University of Michigan—all for cancer research.

The foundation's first non-research project was something of a flop. Gerstacker and his Pardee colleagues were impressed with the work of Dr. Elise L'Esperance at Sloan-Kettering, who "strongly advocated periodic physical examinations for apparently well persons, because early detection of cancer would greatly improve the patient's chances of full recovery," Carl said. Examining healthy people was then a new concept, and it led the Pardee Foundation to initiate cancer detection clinics in Cleveland and Midland, to gauge public reaction to the idea. "The initial interest was excellent," he said, "but the patients, having been informed that they did not have cancer, would not return for regular periodic examinations. The physicians, who provided their services at no charge or less than usual charge, lost their enthusiasm after the examinations became more routine and weren't willing to continue." The detection clinics closed down after a few years even though Dr. L'Esperance's theories about early cancer detection are now generally accepted.

In 1951, his sister Elsa began urging that they do something to help the victims of cancer. "She felt that research was the long-term answer but that many individuals were suffering currently from inadequate medical care for lack of funds, and that something should be done for such unfortunate people while we invested in research at the same time"

"William Allen and Carl Gerstacker disagreed with her," Carl said, "feeling that the problems of determining who should have help, and how much that financial help should

163

be, were completely beyond the ability of the trustees to solve, and would bring about more problems than the trustees could handle. Eda U. Gerstacker joined with Elsa Allen and this major disagreement was decided in favor of doing something for the current victims. Never underestimate the power of mothers and wives."

As a result the Pardee Cancer Treatment Committee was formed as part of the Midland County Cancer Society, with a desk in the Midland Hospital business office, and an initial grant of about $14,000 was made to the committee in 1951. By the early 1980s the committee was spending about $100,000 per year helping the cancer victims of Midland County.

This venture was such a success that in 1975 the assistance program was extended to Brazosport, Texas (covering the area where Dow Chemical has its largest plant), and then in 1977 to Contra Costa County, California (where Dow's Western Division is located), and later on to Bay, Clare, and Isabella Counties in Michigan.

Meanwhile the foundation continued to fund cancer research, primarily at universities and hospitals, and in its first thirty-six years these grants amounted to $9,300,000 to eighty different research organizations. In all the foundation disbursed about $13 million.

Gerstacker was particularly proud of the fact that the total of all the administrative expenses for the first thirty-six years of the foundation were $2,775, or about $77 per year. "The trustees have paid all the expenses except the $2,775," he explained. "The Foundation has expended at least its entire income in each and every year of its existence. It has, in addition, spent about $4 million of its principal."

Throughout those years Gerstacker, as the treasurer, kept the foundation's funds invested exclusively in Dow Chemical common stock, and as he was delighted to point out, the organization's spectacular financial record was "a

great testimony to investing only in Dow Chemical common." The foundation started with 8,000 shares with a market value of $1 million, and at the end of thirty-six years it owned 693,210 shares with a market value of $22,270,000. "Starting with $1 million, it has spent about $13 million and has $22 million left," he said.

By the end of the twentieth century the foundation's assets were hovering around $100 million and it was spending $4 million to $5 million yearly "for the control and cure of cancer." "We must honestly say that we have not accomplished the control and cure of cancer," Gerstacker observed in 1981, "but we have made a major contribution to the knowledge about the disease and the treatment methods. The Foundation has helped cancer victims and their families financially, medically, and psychologically."[2]

After his death in 1995, his fellow trustees established a permanently endowed professorship, honoring his "Unkie" and him, at Case Western Reserve University in Cleveland. The James T. Pardee-Carl A. Gerstacker Professorship in Cancer Research provides significant support for the cancer research program at that university and carries on the work of the Pardee Foundation.

BROAD-GAUGE GIVING

By 1957, when he and his mother founded the Rollin M. Gerstacker Foundation, Carl was ready to leap into the general field of philanthropy with both feet. The Pardee Foundation, with its precise target—"the care and cure of cancer"—did not permit any giving outside that field, and that was only one of the world's problems. His mother was wondering, for example, how they could help the King's Daughters organization build a home for the elderly, badly

needed in Midland. She was making heavy anonymous contributions to help the project along, but it needed more than that. Once mother and son had thought of the answer, it seemed totally logical—set up a new foundation, which they immediately decided they would name in honor of their deceased husband and father, Rollin M. Gerstacker. Its first major project became the building of the King's Daughters Home, for which it provided the lion's share of the cost—$541,000—beginning in 1958.

During the early years it was a modest-sized family foundation, holding its annual and only meeting during the Christmas holidays each year when the family gathered. Frank Harlow, the first non-family trustee, joined the board in 1959 and for the next twenty-seven years was the principal legal adviser of the foundation. That began a slow evolution toward the half-family, half-non-family board that prevails today. Gilbert A. Currie, chairman of Chemical Bank & Trust and also an attorney, and the Reverend Theodore M. Greenhoe, pastor of Memorial Presbyterian Church, joined the board in 1968, and Julius (Jay) Grosberg, a downtown Midland merchant and community activist, in 1973.[3]

Although the composition of the board of trustees changed, the foundation continued to be Gerstacker's creature. He assumed the duties of selecting and nominating new trustees himself, and he was also the Finance Committee and the Investment Committee. He was careful to consult the other trustees before a meeting to solicit their support ahead of time on any matter of particular moment. He kept most of the records of the foundation in a little notebook he carried around, and over the year-end holidays would compile the basic figures for an annual report—required by U.S. law after 1969. As with the Pardee Foundation, the expenses of operating were divided up among the trustees, a practice that faded out with the addition of non-family trustees.

His theory on this matter, developed in long conversations with his mother, was that the maximum percentage of the funds available should be devoted to grants designed "to help people," and the absolute bare minimum devoted to administrative expense. Until 1987, for example, the foundation did not have a telephone listed in its name. "If you had a telephone," Gerstacker reasoned, "that meant you'd need someone to answer the telephone, and that meant you'd have to have paid staff," which he wished at all costs to avoid.

The foundation continues today, in the Gerstacker mold, to have no paid staff except for a part-time administrative assistant.

When he and his mother sat down to define their purpose for the foundation, they made it very simple—"to carry on indefinitely financial aid to charities of all types supported by Mr. and Mrs. R. M. Gerstacker during their lifetimes."

Most notably this mandate covers the following: (1) housing for the elderly, for which the foundation continues to play a leadership role, especially in the Midland area; (2) support for almost any project aimed at the betterment of life in the Midland area, ranging from the building of golf courses to improvement of the city's downtown area; (3) support of the Midland school system and of a wide range of colleges and universities, especially those supplying large numbers of graduates to Midland and Dow Chemical; and (4) social services for young people and those with special needs. There are few things having to do with the betterment of Midland that cannot be squeezed under the umbrella of the foundation in one way or another, giving the trustees a great deal of latitude in their choices for making grants as well as allowing for changing situations over long periods of time.

For instance, in the early years the foundation was a substantial supporter of the Gerstacker family church, Memorial Presbyterian in Midland, but with the passage of time and a

167

greatly diversified board of directors the foundation was as likely to support a Jewish or Catholic cause as any other. Indeed, it has now stopped giving to religious organizations almost entirely.

In 2002 the foundation published the first compiled record of its giving and activities, together with a brief history of the organization. By then it had passed the $100 million mark in total giving, had assets in excess of $200 million, and was among the ten largest foundations in Michigan. It grew substantially with two major bequests: the first from Eda Gerstacker when she died in 1975—its first major addition, amounting to $20 million; and the second from Carl when he died in 1995.

POLITICS

The stepfather-stepson relationship is a terribly difficult one, not always easy to work out. Gerstacker's stepson, Bill Schuette (b. 1953), was still a student when Carl Gerstacker married his mother, and as happens with many only sons, he was the apple of his mother's eye. It was not as if they were strangers. Bill's earliest memory of the man who became his stepfather was being invited to dinner at the Gerstackers as a little boy. He did not like the green peas he was served, and Carl, laughing, showed the child how to hide peas inside the mashed potatoes. Later on, after Bill's father died, Gerstacker occasionally took the boy along with him to football games in Ann Arbor or Detroit. Gerstacker also taught him such male essentials as how to play craps.

In 1979 Bill graduated from law school (Georgetown and San Francisco) and decided, bitten early by the political bug, to go to work for George H. W. Bush, who ten years later would become president. This precipitated their first violent

quarrel. Gerstacker thought the idea of working for George Bush was "absolutely nuts" and adamantly opposed it. He and some of his colleagues were backing John Connally of Texas for the presidency. Why didn't Bill go to work for John Connally? Young Schuette stuck to his guns and worked on the Bush campaign in Michigan. Eight years later he became manager of the Bush campaign in Florida—in 1988 Schuette was again backing George Bush, while Gerstacker and his friends were backing Jack Kemp. When Bush was elected president, Gerstacker sent young Bill a note saying, "You were right about Bush—you're a better politician than I am."

In 1984 Bill decided he was ready to launch his own political career, and announced he was running for Congress from his home district in central Michigan. The incumbent there was Don Albosta, of St. Charles, Michigan, a Democrat and a veteran campaigner in the political wars. Albosta had served several terms in the House of Representatives and expected to serve several more. Most of the pundits considered him a shoo-in for re-election. Young Schuette leaped at the chance to run against him.

"Going into August our campaign was in disarray, to say the least," Schuette said. "We were just flat out disorganized. We desperately needed someone to take hold of it and run it." That "someone" became his stepfather, Carl Gerstacker, who dropped everything else and ran Schuette's campaign for the last few critical months in the stretch run to the election. Schuette's two sisters (Sandra, who lived in Connecticut, and Gretchen, who lived in Oregon) both came back to Michigan and worked on the campaign for periods of time, Gretchen in spite of the fact that she was a Democrat.

Thus, overnight, Gerstacker became a political campaign manager. Every Friday morning he held a strategy meeting with Schuette, Alan Ott (chairman of Chemical Bank in Midland), and Dennis Starner, a veteran political adviser. "It

169

was a whole education to see Carl tangle with the young Turks of the Republican party," Sandra (Schuette) Joys said.

Myles Martel, of Philadelphia, a highly successful professional debate and speaking coach, probably best known as Pres. Ronald Reagan's debate coach, said Gerstacker, a total stranger, came to see him during that 1984 campaign. His stepson, Bill Schuette, needed some training for TV appearances and debates and the like, he told Martel, and Martel had been recommended as a trainer. Martel asked who he was. Gerstacker said he was retired. From what company? Dow Chemical. What did you do there? "I was in finance." Gerstacker never let on that he was the board chairman, which Martel of course found out eventually. Martel took on the job of training Schuette and they did a lot of role-playing. They needed someone to play the role of Albosta, so Gerstacker became Albosta. "He did a fantastic job of playing Don Albosta," Martel said.

170

(In a later campaign, in 1990, when Schuette ran for the U.S. Senate against Sen. Carl Levin, Martel again helped with the training and in that campaign, Gerstacker played the role of Carl Levin. But Senator Levin trounced Schuette in that one.)

The 1984 campaign went down to the wire. It was nip and tuck, and the result was not clear until 4 A.M. the next morning, with Schuette declared the winner by a narrow margin. Gerstacker had made up a chart of the congressional district township by township, showing Schuette's vote expectations in each one, and they spent most of the night, as results came in, comparing the results with their "expectations." The results were so close that Albosta asked for a recount, and Gerstacker then took on the massive chore of lining up people at each polling place in the district to represent Schuette at the recount. Schuette won by 1,314 votes. "I would not have won without Carl's help," Schuette said.

"When he had a disagreement with me, and we had a lot of them, he would have a piece of paper in his hand—sometimes he'd give it to you afterward, sometimes not—on which he had written down where you were right, and where you were wrong, and how bad, and how wrong, and he would read it off to you," Schuette said. "This was always a tough kind of session, sometimes unpleasant, but always helpful."

After Senator Levin drubbed him in the 1990 elections, Schuette went into Michigan governor John Engler's "cabinet" as the state director of agriculture. In 1993 he received a message that Gerstacker was on his way to Lansing and wanted to see him. Gerstacker told Bill, "I think you should run for the State Senate." Schuette did, and won, and came to the term limits of his tenure as a state senator at the end of 2002. In November 2002, he ran for the State Court of Appeals, was elected, and made a successful transition to the bench.

"He never refused to help me, in my campaigns or otherwise," Schuette said. "He taught me political fundraising. He always made his own phone calls. He never asked anyone else to make phone calls for him. He was a modest man, but powerful, and he always told me, 'Don't act like a big shot.' If he ordered a drink he would order 'gin and tonic.' If I ordered a 'Tanqueray gin and tonic' he would tell me, 'You're trying to be a big shot. Don't act like a big shot.' He always made it a point to refer to me as 'our son,' just as my sisters were always 'our daughters.' If you did something he really approved of he was careful to tell you about it." When Bill married Cynthia Grebe, a Midland girl who had become a TV news broadcaster in Grand Rapids, Gerstacker told him, "Bill, marrying Cynthia is the best decision you ever made."

When Schuette ran against Senator Levin, Gerstacker opposed the whole idea as violently as he could, and they had serious arguments about it. But after the election was over and Schuette was feeling as though he had been completely

171

crushed, Gerstacker sought him out and told him, "Bill, it's not the end of the world. I didn't get to be president of Dow, you know. We all lose some."

GETTING THINGS DONE

The relationship between Carl Gerstacker and Herbert H. Dow II ranged from love to hate and back again. Herb, grandson of the founder Herbert Dow, was for many years president of the Herbert H. & Grace A. Dow Foundation, by far the largest among the fifteen or sixteen foundations in Midland, and Carl was the leader of the Gerstacker Foundation, the second largest. Herb was also the largest shareholder of the Dow company, its corporate secretary, and a longtime member of its board of directors.

Sometimes they were the best of friends, sometimes the worst of enemies. Sometimes they got along like the lifelong friends they were, and at other times they could not abide each other. When they worked together they could accomplish almost anything, but when they opposed each other it usually meant nothing much was going to happen.

Frank Popoff, who knew both men well, said, "Carl was never willing to lose control. Herb had a big heart but was inconsistent and undisciplined, and it was sometimes hard to get the two of them on the same page."[4]

Probably the greatest monument to their ability to work together is the Midland Foundation, which has also been known as the Midland Area Foundation and is now known as the Midland Area Community Foundation. That foundation came about as the result of one of the original efforts to beautify the city, beginning in 1973.

When the I-75 superhighway—running from Key West, Florida, all the way to the Straits of Mackinac—was routed

through Michigan in the late 1960s it skirted delicately around the city of Midland and continued on its scenic way north, toward the Upper Peninsula of the state. Provisions were left for a spur that would enter the city proper from the expressway and make its way to the downtown area. As a result the main entrance to the city from the populous southeastern portion of Michigan wound through the poorest and most rundown area of the town. Eventually, wending his way through an urban wasteland, the visitor would arrive at the imposing, new Midland Center for the Arts, the big, new Grace A. Dow Library, and the city's top tourist attraction, the Dow Gardens. Reporters and writers visiting these places began to comment on the ugliness of the city's entryway.

"This is terrible," said Herb Dow. "We've got to do something about it." "This is terrible," said Carl Gerstacker. "We've got to do something about it." After several conversations they agreed to tackle the problem. They talked to their colleagues at the Dow company and to representatives of the State Highway Department and drew up a map following the route into town. Over the next few years, they agreed, they would buy up the dilapidated old houses along this route, tear them down, and build a greenway that led all the way from the expressway to downtown Midland. Their map showed which parcels they would need to buy, and the Dow company quickly agreed that the property it owned along the proposed greenway would be made available for this project.

173

As they talked about their project it began to grow. The downtown riverfront area of the city also had a lot of eyesores, and a riverfront beautification project began to look like a logical companion piece to the greenbelt. It too would take a few years to clean up. Eventually they arrived at a gentlemen's agreement—the Dow Foundation would put up the money to buy up the properties for the greenway property entering the city, and take the lead in that project, and the Gerstacker

Foundation would develop and fund the riverfront develop-ment, and take the lead in that project.

As they developed their ideas it became apparent that they would need a manager to negotiate the purchase of properties and take care of all sorts of other details. Since family foundations did not have the personnel to buy or man-age property, Gerstacker raised the idea of a community foun-dation. "We have one down in Cleveland," he said, "and their whole intent is community improvement, which they accom-plish by soliciting the contributions of local people and using them for specific improvement projects." Dow said that he had heard of community foundations and that might be exactly what they were looking for.

In relatively short order they had organized the Midland Community Foundation. They talked with other community leaders—Cliff Miles, the city manager, Ned S. Arbury, of Arbury Insurance and a long-time community leader—and began to collect names of people who might be candidates to serve on a board of trustees representing a broad cross sec-tion of the community.

O. James Clark, a school official, became the first presi-dent, and Esther Gerstacker the first vice president. The board soon hired its first executive director, the Reverend Wayne R. North, recently retired as minister of the First United Methodist Church on Main Street. North had suffered a heart attack and had retired on medical advice, but had clearance to take on a part-time job and was delighted with this one. Ned Arbury provided an office in a building at 115 Jerome, and Dr. North was soon at work buying up properties in the greenbelt area and tearing them down. Herbert Dow and the Dow Foundation set up a $10 million fund which it put at the disposal of the Midland Foundation to develop the greenbelt. Eventually, some ten years later, that project was completed and the city had a parkland type of entry all the

way from the expressway to the downtown area, a distance of some four miles.

That was the first task of the Midland Foundation, which proceeded from that beginning to grow into one of the state's biggest and best community foundations, with assets at the turn of the century of about $50 million.

Meanwhile, Carl Gerstacker was working—behind the scenes, largely—on the problems of beautifying the Midland riverfront. The old Benson Street Bridge came down, and the new Mark Putnam Bridge went up. The wetlands across the river, which flooded almost every spring, were gradually cleared of residences and refashioned into sports grounds and parkland. An old grain silo alongside Benson Street, unused for years, finally came down. A new farmer's market was built at the foot of Ashman Street and provided with ample new parking lots.

A key element in the cleanup of the riverfront area was the sale and demolition of the old Brown Lumber Company, the major remaining business establishment in the area, and its purchase by the Midland Foundation. Roy B. Lanham, its proprietor, was one of the community leaders involved in the foundation, and was fully cognizant of and sympathetic to this development. He and Gerstacker negotiated the transaction.

175

The demolition of the lumber company, coupled with the demolition of the old J. C. Penney store on Main Street, made room for a hotel on Main Street which everyone agreed was the city's most urgent need. Building a hotel on Main Street became something of a passion with Gerstacker. Opponents pointed out to him all the legal impossibilities of building a hotel with charitable foundation backing and the backing of a chemical company, but he persisted. "We're a world class company and we need a world class town," he argued

Eventually the Marriott Ashman Court hotel was built where the J. C. Penney store had stood through a complex

legal instrument that provided backing from Midland foundations as well as guarantees that Dow would use its conference center and other facilities. In later years Gerstacker and Herb Dow found ways to use the fledgling Midland Foundation that they established for myriad other purposes aimed at the improvement of their town. "The Midland Foundation is primarily a vehicle for getting things done," Carl said.

BARLEY MACTAVISH

Gerstacker had been initiated into the joys of anonymous giving both by his mother, who preferred to remain incognito in many of her charities—the King's Daughters Home was only one of them—and by his Uncle Jim, who on occasion also preferred to remain unknown to his beneficiaries.[5] When Carl made cash gifts (sometimes they were called "loans") to needy friends or relatives, it was always an anonymous act.

Every year, for example, he sent a check for $1,000 to each of the Dow plant managers around the country with instructions to donate it to a local charity of the manager's choice. He reasoned that the manager would know the local situation and needs far better than he would.

Probably his most ambitious project as an anonymous giver was worked out in conversations with his good friend, Norman C. (Slim) Rumple, the long-time editor of the *Midland Daily News*. He and Slim were both active in the Masonic order, and after they retired the two of them were the spearheads of the Main Street Coffee Club, over which Slim presided for many years. It was and is a club maintained by the city's retired leaders which meets every weekday morning at 9:45 for a cup of coffee and discussion of the day's events and the city's problems.

Slim mentioned the many letters the newspaper received from local citizens who had problems involving relatively small amounts of money—utilities turned off because of bills not paid, automobiles broken down and no money to fix them, medical care put off for lack of funds, household facilities needing repairs—the list seemed endless. He was constantly surprised, Slim said, by the frequency with which such problems turned up in a prosperous community such as Midland, "mostly problems that could be fixed up with a few hundred bucks."

"Suppose I gave you a few hundred," Gerstacker suggested. "Could you take care of the problem and keep me out of it?" This conversation led to others, and eventually to a proposal whereby Gerstacker would from time to time put "a few thousand" dollars into a special fund at the newspaper which would be used to "solve problems." The newspaper's readers would be encouraged to write the paper about their problems, or those of their relatives or friends, and a staff writer would look into the "problems" and make recommendations on expenditures from the fund to Gerstacker, who would approve (or disapprove) the expenditure and the amount. The beneficiary's request letter would then be printed in the newspaper, with a response from the paper. Gerstacker's role in funding the program would be carefully concealed, and the gifts ascribed simply to "an anonymous donor."

177

The newspaper proposed to give a fictitious name to the anonymous donor, and asked Gerstacker for a nom de plume. The newspaper would have a cartoonist sketch this imaginary person and the name and cartoon would then be used to identify the program and be printed with the letters and responses.

Gerstacker immediately came up with the name "Barley"—the name Gerstacker, in German, meant "barley

field." He talked to Esther about it, who would approve grants from the fund in his absence. Since Esther had always liked the name "MacTavish" which occurred in her family, "Barley MacTavish" was born.[6]

Since then Barley MacTavish has been a popular and regular feature of the *Midland Daily News*. (Esther continued to fund the program after Carl's death.) "Barley MacTavish, problem solver, invites readers to write to him about themselves or other people," the column is regularly introduced, "explaining why they need help and what they have tried to do about their problems. Write to Barley, care of the *Midland Daily News*, at Box 432, Midland, MI 48640, and be sure to include a telephone number."

"There is no real Barley MacTavish," the newspaper explains. "He is an anonymous donor who relishes his privacy. His financial support, plus donations from area residents during the holiday season, makes this column possible. Barley is undertaking this project, he says, to help make Midland a little better place to live."

178

UNITED WAY

In the fall of 1981, having retired at his sixty-fifth birthday in August, he turned to one of his favorite charitable efforts, the United Way, and took on the daunting task of guiding its annual funding campaign that fall. He had been president of the Midland Community Fund (as it was then called) twenty-eight years before, in 1953, and the fund had raised $128,857 during its annual fall campaign that year. Now he faced the challenge of raising $1.5 million, which the Midland Community Fund had raised in 1980—the largest sum ever raised.

Looking through the statistics for United Way campaigns around the country, he found an even greater challenge. The

national leader in per-capita giving, he discovered, was none other than Cleveland, his old home town, and he quickly decided that the real challenge was to outdo Cleveland, and that became his target for the 1981 campaign—to bring Midland giving up to a level where it was the highest per-capita United Way agency in the country.

He probably worked as hard on that campaign as he had on any fundraising campaign he had ever been involved in. When the results were in, they showed that the Midland United Way had increased its total giving by a whopping twenty-one percent over the year before to $1,877,045—the highest increase the agency had ever recorded. When all the numbers were in it also turned out that he had led Midland to the record as the highest per-capita United Way in the country, beating out Cleveland, the perennial leader.

Twenty years later, Midland is still a national leader in fundraising, coming in third in per-capita giving in 2001 after Winston-Salem and Seattle.[7]

There was also an unspoken challenge for him in this campaign. Esther had been president of the United Way a few years before, and with David L. Rooke as campaign chairman had for the first time raised more than $1 million for the Midland United Way in 1977. The challenge to him, of course, was to do better than she had done.

THE FLOOD

Valley Drive meanders through Midland for about a mile, twisting and turning all the way, running through grassy parkland from the Midland Hospital at its northern end to the municipal Midland cemetery at its southern . It traces in some street-namer's imagination the "valley" of Sturgeon Creek, a brush-choked little stream which Valley Drive struggles

valiantly to follow. The Gerstacker house stands about midway in its course. It is one of the streets of Midland's upper crust, peopled with Dow Chemical executives and Herbert Dow's descendants and an occasional doctor or lawyer.

In normal times Sturgeon Creek is a peaceful stream, although almost every spring it overflows its banks a few days with melting snow before it turns placid again. In water-expert lore the creek, and the Tittabawassee River into which it flows, should generate a real flood only once every 500 years, and that's what it did in September 1986.

The Gerstackers arrived home about midnight on 12 September from a trip to the Far East, and bone-weary from the long voyage went right to bed. Esther looked out the window and said, "My goodness, the water is up to the window sills." Carl said, "That's all right. Let's go to bed. I'm tired." "I think we ought to get things out of the living room," Esther said. But Carl replied, "No, we're going to bed."[8]

About 3:00 A.M. the telephone was ringing, and it was a neighbor, Donna McArdle Carl, calling, and the water was almost knee-deep in the bedroom. "Esther," Donna said, "you're the only house on this whole street that isn't lighted up. What's the matter? Don't you know you have to get out? You have to evacuate."

"So we got up and we started to work and we worked until 2 o'clock in the afternoon," Esther said,

> taking things up off the floor and putting them wherever we could. We don't have a basement and we don't have an attic so we had a problem. So we put them on the highest pieces of furniture that we possibly could. One couch we lifted and put on two chairs which was a great effort for me, I must tell you. But that didn't really help much. We lost all of our furniture except for the one large dining-room table. We were able to keep that and a few pieces of furniture we had redone. I guess they are

all right but I still think they are never going to be quite the same. All the woodwork had to be done over because of all the built-in features of the Alden Dow type of house. . . .

I lost all of the mementoes that were in the store room because that was on a lower level, like the living room. We lost all of the pictures and books and things we had kept from the early days of everyone, of our college days, and so forth. We lost all of that and many pictures of my mother and father. . . .

When they finally left, Carl took their two large dogs and waded out with the two dogs on leashes, swimming in places. Esther's son, Bill Schuette, and his friend Dave Camp came and took Esther out in a canoe. The floodwater was about three feet deep throughout the house. "The firewood from the fireplace was in our beds," she said, "so you know things were floating. We had an unbelievable time."

It was about March 1987, before they were able to move back into the house. "We were lucky to have a place to stay, however," she said. "It was on Michigan Street. We got so we liked it and it was real easy to take care of it. It was about one big room and two bedrooms, and very small bedrooms and hard beds you could fall off of—I had to go tippy-toe to get up on the bed. That was a very nice house and we were very lucky to get it. . . . Everyday and early I would have to go over to the old house and see what else I could do. Finding a good decorator was impossible because everyone wanted a decorator—they were in great demand."

"It was wonderful to get back into my own home."

181

9

THE BELOVED CITY, 1987–95

1989 Is named a Paul Harris Fellow by the Midland Rotary Club.

Begins a two-year stint teaching business classes to sixth graders at Carpenter School, Midland.

In November, construction begins on the Carl A. Gerstacker Building at the Midland County Fairgrounds, named in his honor for his contributions to the fairgrounds, and it is completed in time for the annual fair in August 1990.

1990 Carl and Esther Gerstacker are chosen honorary chairpersons of the Michigan Council of Foundations for its annual gathering.

1991 Chairs annual fund drive for Junior Achievement of Midland. Begins work on conversion of railroad tracks westward from Midland into a "rail trail."

1992 Is first recipient of the newly established University of Michigan Engineering Alumni Society Medal.

In June, when he complains of constant tiredness, doctors give him a series of tests and diagnose chronic lymphocytic leukemia, or CLL ("blood cancer," he calls it). They inform him he probably has only a few months to live—"more, if he's lucky." He shares this news quite calmly with family and close friends. Subsequently, receives frequent blood transfusions, following which he feels reinvigorated, but as time goes on this becomes less and less frequent and effective.

1993 Is named (along with his wife) honorary sheriff's deputy by Sheriff John Reder of Midland.

Riverside Place, new senior citizen residence for which he is largely responsible, opens on Midland's Main Street.

1994 Doctors advise him to avoid crowds because of his extreme susceptibility to cold germs. He is soon living in virtual isolation in his hospital room.

184

1995   On 24 February, last public appearance, at the Main Street Coffee Club, a Midland organization he has fostered and enjoyed for many years.

On 14 March enters hospital for last time. Dies in Midland hospital 23 April. Buried in Midland Cemetery 26 April.

1996   On 28 September, about forty of his friends and family gather for a "memorial celebration" in the grove of redwoods he owned near Mendocino, California. He has left funds in his will to pay for this event.

CARL AND ESTHER HAD PLANNED TO MOVE TO "A NICE warm climate" when he retired, probably to the place he had built on St. John in the Caribbean, but when it came time to move they decided they did not want to leave Midland. "There were just too many things pulling us back," Gerstacker said. "I think Midland is the finest place in the world to live."

Instead he threw himself into remaking the town they loved, and he spent an increasing amount of his time and money on the beautification and revitalization of his home city, and especially on the heart of the city, its downtown. "You've got to stay busy," he said. "You have to find something that gives you a feeling of accomplishment."[1]

"I used to wonder why it was that Herbert Dow tried so hard to make Midland into a fine place to live," he told an interviewer. "He did so many things to provide community services for people—the library, the community center. He brought a Japanese gardener to town, for example, and made him available to anyone who wanted to improve his yard or his garden—the Japanese fellow would give the person free advice."

"Midland was a terrible place to live when Herbert Dow came to town," Gerstacker said. "It was a leftover lumbering town, dying on its feet, and Main Street was mainly drinking places. I finally got through my thick skull that the reason he was doing all this was that he wanted to bring the best people he could find to Midland, the best chemists, the best people for his company, and the only way he could get them to come here and stay here was if this was a good place to live. Herbert Dow was really doing this as a matter of his own self-interest, but it took me awhile to realize that."

"I saw downtown Cleveland decaying," he said, "and I began to wonder, why should we worry about the downtown area of Cleveland or any other city? And I wondered, why worry

about downtown Midland? There are perhaps other areas of the city that might replace the downtown, and I did a lot of soul-searching about that. I decided the downtown of any town is the heart of the town, and you can't grow a new one. The downtown is one of the most important parts of any town."[2]

In 1985, authorized to do so by a new state law, the city established a new Downtown Development Authority with the specific mission of improving the downtown area, and he became one of its charter members, working with the municipal authorities and interested citizens to remove the heavy blight that had invaded Midland's downtown.

In the next few years he was involved in a continuing series of ventures to improve the downtown area—to make it "world class," as he put it:

- Beginning with the purchase of the Brown Lumber Company and the J. C. Penney store, he acquired contiguous properties and pushed for the building of what is now the Ashman Court hotel, which occupies a full city block, lining up the financial backing of the Dow Chemical Company and other local interests in order to attract a major hotel chain (Marriott) to the area.
- Also on Main Street, he acquired more properties and built a major office building in the downtown area. The building is now owned jointly (49 percent each) by the Midland Community Foundation and the Downtown Development Authority, with the remaining one percent owned by a management firm, the Acquest Corporation.
- When it became apparent that a large office building in the downtown area would require a companion parking facility to be successful, he acquired another large chunk of nearby property and proceeded to construct a two-story downtown parking facility.

187

- When the Sears Company decided to build a large store at the new Midland Mall, out of town, leaving its big downtown store deserted on Main Street, Gerstacker and others—the Strosacker Foundation took the lead—organized a campaign to find a new use for the place. Remodeled and renovated, it became the headquarters of Midland's United Way and related organizations.
- When Midland's last five-and-dime store closed its doors, leaving another glaring gap on Main Street, Gerstacker and others looked for a suitable tenant and found one, the Mackinac Center for Public Policy. With the support, again, of the city's major foundations, the building was completely remodeled.
- A messy tangle of empty storefronts at the eastern end of Main Street was removed and in 1993 became the site of the city's largest senior citizen residence, called Riverside Place. The site and the building were funded by the foundations, the Gerstacker Foundation taking the lead with a gift of $4.4 million—its largest grant to that time.
- With most of the sidewalks in the downtown area torn up for these and other projects, Gerstacker was one of the leaders in instituting what was called a "cityscape" program—i.e., replacing the walks in the downtown area with new, attractive, patterned walkways.
- When the Pere Marquette railroad decided to cease rail traffic west of Midland (it maintained and maintains the tracks in an easterly direction as far as the Dow Chemical Company), the tracks were unused and deserted from downtown Midland all the way west to Lake Michigan. In various parts of the nation where this also occurred the tracks were being made into "rail trails" and Gerstacker, acquainted with railroad affairs through his service on one of the railroad boards of

directors (Conrail Corporation), initiated a program to purchase and pave the rail trail from Midland to Clare for the account of the Midland Community Foundation—a task that took three years to accomplish. The Pere Marquette Rail Trail begins in downtown Midland and stretches north and west to Clare. Still growing along the path once followed by the locomotives, the trail today is one of the area's most popular attractions for hikers, bikers, joggers, and inline skaters.

As broadly as he could, Gerstacker stressed what he called "challenge grants" in building these projects. "Wide participation is necessary to a good community project," he said. "Unless people support the project it won't last long. I don't really appreciate and use things that people give me, and most people are that way. If I haven't put some of my own self and my own money in it I tend not to appreciate it."

The "Tridge," a three-legged bridge at the junction of the Chippewa and Tittabawassee Rivers, where the city was originally settled, was a good example of this, in his opinion. The cost to build such a bridge was estimated at $732,000. The Gerstacker Foundation announced that it would supply half this sum, or $366,000, if the community would match that amount.

189

"People in Midland feel as if the Tridge is theirs," Esther said. "Why? Because just about everyone in town contributed to the building of it. Everything they gave was matched dollar for dollar by the Gerstacker Foundation. Children came in carrying bags of pennies they collected. I remember one boy bringing in a bag of 40,000 pennies, I think it was. It was the first time he realized just how heavy 40,000 pennies can be."

"Foundations have money but no people," Carl said. "Most communities have a lot of needs but not enough money to take care of them. That's where the foundations come in. It

would be a mistake for foundations just to do big projects like the Tridge. There has to be backing of them by the people."

The fundraising drive for the Tridge brought in $368,000, more than was needed, and the structure was opened in 1981. Since that time it has become something of a symbol for the city. "It has become the centerpiece that ties the community together," said Cliff Miles, city manager at the time it was built. "It serves as the focal point for festivals, family outings, concerts and other events, and brings thousands of residents and visitors to the area every year. It has revitalized the downtown area."[3]

THUNDERCLAP

"It was like a thunderclap, only not loud," Gerstacker said, "a sort of inner thunderclap," when he learned that he had not long to live. He had been complaining to his family physician, Dr. Christopher Hough, a Midland gerontologist, that he was feeling tired—"I'm tired all the time, even after a good night's sleep," he told him. Dr. Hough advised a series of tests, including blood studies.

When the results were in, he told him it was bad news. "I'm afraid you have a rather rare condition called 'chronic lymphocytic leukemia,'" he said. "It's a sort of blood cancer, in lay terms. And what is even worse, there's no cure for it."

"How long do I have to live?" Gerstacker asked.

"I have to give you the straight answer to that," Dr. Hough said. "You may last only a few months—six months, maybe. With good care and good luck, yes, it could be longer than that—how much longer, I don't know."

This happened in June 1992. He was soon under the care of a cancer specialist, Dr. Lijda Vellekoop, and for the rest of his life—thirty-four months, as it turned out—he was in and

out of a hospital room at the Mid-Michigan Regional Medical Center.

His family and close friends remembered that he came and told them about his medical condition, one at a time, somberly, in private. "He dropped by and said he had something to tell me," one friend remembered. "He said he had received a terrible medical report and that he had blood cancer and probably only had a few months to live. He was very matter-of-fact about it, and in five minutes he was gone. I sat there stunned, trying to measure the impact of what he had said." Bill Schuette, his stepson, said he had the same kind of experience.

At intervals he would receive a massive blood transfusion, and when he did he immediately felt strong and alert. On these occasions he would invariably head directly from the transfusion to the Midland Tennis Center for a game with whatever friendly opponent he happened to find there. "Slow down, for heaven's sake," Esther told him. "I need the exercise," he said. "I haven't been getting any exercise."

191

He also went to an office he had maintained at the Chemical Bank & Trust Company, in downtown Midland, since his retirement, and sorted through his mail. And he frequented as well his office at the Gerstacker Foundation, where he worked on foundation affairs, reviewing the requests for funding that kept coming in.

In these final years of philanthropic activity he began to prefer giving to rural volunteer groups, and especially to volunteer fire departments, which were generally looking to buy a new fire engine. After his death, the foundation discovered that he had talked to volunteer fire departments throughout the Midwest about their needs for shiny new red fire engines.

He had an arrangement with Esther whereby he would peel apples for apple pie on fall Saturdays while watching college football games on TV and she would not bother him

about it. They were both happy with the arrangement. "That was the first signal that something was wrong," said his step-daughter Sandra, "when he stopped peeling those apples."

A year before, in 1991, he had served as fundraising chairman for Junior Achievement of Midland, and it was the last time he was able physically to manage such activity. He had always been a stalwart supporter of JA, and had served on its board of directors in Midland for eighteen years.

The honors continued to pile up. In 1992 the University of Michigan Engineering School established its Alumni Society Medal, and Gerstacker was the first recipient. It became the occasion for his last visit to his alma mater. In 1993, in recognition of his initiation of and long-standing support of the Midland Law Enforcement Awards—he had established them in 1966—he and Esther were named honorary sheriff's deputies by Midland's veteran county sheriff, John S. Reder. (The awards are conferred annually on outstanding police and sheriff's officers in Midland). After the twenty-eighth annual awards had been given, the sheriff called the Gerstackers to the podium and swore them in as honorary deputies.

"They've been great supporters of law enforcement in Midland County for many years," Reder said. "We decided it was time for us to do something for them."

"All we try to do is thank the officers for the wonderful jobs they do," Gerstacker said. "There was no need for anything from them."[4]

His health sank slowly throughout the year of 1994 and by the beginning of 1995 he was unable to make out checks any more. He turned this chore over to Bill Schuette. "The biggest compliment he could pay anyone, I think, was letting me pay his bills when he couldn't do it anymore," Bill said. "My last memory of him is of the two of us sitting in the hospital room watching *Rocky,* the Sly Stallone movie, on TV while I balanced his checkbook."[5]

The doctors warned him about his extreme susceptibility to colds and pulmonary diseases and told him to stay away from crowds, where he was apt to pick up stray germs of one kind or another. He did, and soon was turning away visitors even when they were close friends.

On 14 March, St. Patrick's Day, he entered the hospital for the last time. He had caught what he thought was a cold, but it kept getting worse. Dr. Vellekoop diagnosed it as pulmonary aspergillosis and was unhappy about it. "I was afraid something like that would happen," she said.

As he sank toward death his visitors were restricted to immediate family and the Reverend Wallace H. (Wally) Mayton III, a Presbyterian clergyman and close friend. "His last days were peaceful," Wally said later, "and he left this earth in a peaceful frame of mind, at peace with his God. He felt at the end that he still had so much to do, but he accepted that his time was up."[6]

As he lay dying there was a knock on the door, and Bill Schuette answered it to find Dr. Eldon Bailey at the door. "I'm sorry, Eldon," Bill said, "no visitors are allowed except immediate family." "God sent me," Eldon said, and Bill let him enter. Eldon and Carl had been fellow Sunday school teachers at Memorial Presbyterian many years before and Eldon, an intensely religious man, had become his longtime friend—and dentist. Eldon said God had let him know Carl was dying and had laid it on his heart to pray with him for the salvation of his soul before he did. Carl said, "Thank you, Eldon, I'm glad you came." The two men prayed quietly together, and Eldon left.

Shortly after that, at ten minutes past 11 P.M., Carl Gerstacker went to his eternal sleep. It was 23 April 1995. His last words, Esther said, were, "Don't worry—I'll be all right."

Dr. Vellekoop, who had the sorrowful duty of making out the death certificate, listed pulmonary aspergillosis as the cause of death, as a consequence of chronic lymphocytic

193

leukemia, with staphylococcus bacteremia as a heavily contributing factor.[7]

IN MEMORIAM

The Dow board of directors, at its first meeting following Gerstacker's death, adopted a resolution in his memory which read as follows:

> Whereas, our friend and colleague, Carl A. Gerstacker, director emeritus and senior statesman of our Company, departed this life on April 23, 1995; and
>
> Whereas, Carl Gerstacker was for a generation the guiding financial genius of our Company, serving his apprenticeship at the knee of Earl Bennett and becoming assistant treasurer in 1948 when only 32 years old, serving as treasurer for 10 years, and serving as member of our finance committee for an unparalleled 33 years and as its Chairman for 22, earning for the Company and himself a degree of respect on Wall Street seldom equaled in our time; and
>
> Whereas, as a member of the 'troika' that guided our Company's destinies so successfully for so many years, during which time he was Chairman of the Board, he and his partners Ted Doan and Ben Branch provided the Company with a quality of leadership that was long the delight of our Company's shareholders and the envy of others in American industry; and
>
> Whereas, through his deep and loving involvement in the community of Midland, his chosen dwelling place, to which with his wife Esther he devoted time and substance in full measure, he established standards of humanitarianism and philanthropy that will stand permanently for the guidance of his successors in the Company.
>
> Now Therefore, Be It Resolved, that this Board records its

sorrow at his passing and expresses its resolve to remember and to seek to emulate the spirit of stewardship with which he always conducted himself, and the basic Gerstacker principles of sound finance; and

Be It Further Resolved, that a copy of this resolution be conveyed to Esther Gerstacker and the family as an expression of this Board's faithful and enduring memories of its departed member and Chairman.

It was signed for the board by Frank Popoff, chairman and CEO, and William S. Stavropoulos, president and chief operating officer.[8]

CELEBRATION IN THE SEQUOIAS

Carl Gerstacker's last will and testament, and the U.S. estate tax return disposing of his assets, is a fat document a full inch-and-a-half thick composed of several hundred pages of legalese language and tax forms, but buried in it is a paragraph of pure Gerstacker prose that is quite extraordinary, expressing his last wish for his family and friends.

"Fate has been kind to me, and my life has been a happy one, primarily because of a multitude of friends," Gerstacker wrote in this section.

195

> My death should not be a solemn or sad occasion for family or friends. I would like them to be upbeat and happy. I therefore instruct the trustee to expend as an expense of administration up to $50,000 of my trust estate in payment of all expenses relating to a celebration with food, drink and music. The trustee shall consult with my stepson, William Duncan Schuette, who shall be the exclusive and complete authority to determine the time, location, invitees, arrangements, and all other details

relating to this celebration; provided, that in all events, the celebration shall take place no later than three months following my death after which time amounts, if any, not expended nor set aside for payment from the foregoing sum shall be disposed of as part of my residuary trust estate. I certainly hope everyone has a wonderful time![9]

Schuette said his stepfather had told him, "Bill, you're good at throwing parties. When I die I want you to give a party."

"Wouldn't that be a little odd," Bill asked, "throwing a party because you died?" They discussed it pro and con and back and forth, with Gerstacker still contending that he wanted a party. Finally he said, "Bill, I'll provide the money for it, and you do whatever you think is best."[10]

The party, the family decided, should take place in the redwood grove at Mendocino, his favorite place on this earth, with the guests housed at the Little River Inn, and it would have to take place late in the season, when the Little River Inn would be able to provide accommodations for the visitors; during the busy season there was literally no room at the inn. There was also a consensus that throwing a party just a few weeks after the funeral "didn't seem right." "There's no rush," Bill and Esther felt, "let's wait a bit."

That violated the "no later than three months following my death" stipulation in his will—the party actually took place seventeen months after his death—but they were sure he would understand. Sandra Schuette Joys, his stepdaughter, took charge of most of the arrangements.[11]

"You are invited to a celebration in the redwoods," the invitations read, "in memory of Carl A. Gerstacker, as a guest of his family, September 27, 28, and 29, 1996." The weekend began with cocktails and an informal barbecue on Friday evening as the guests gathered at Little River, and continued

196

on Saturday with the main event, a picnic in the redwoods. Tables with sparkling white linen and china were set out under the towering sequoias, which in all their hundreds of years of existence had surely not seen anything like it. Grills were set up to serve a menu he would have loved, featuring Ball Park hot dogs and brownies, specifically the gooey type.

About forty of his family and friends gathered for the event. Almost all of them had participated, over the years, in Carl Gerstacker's annual sprucing up of his redwood grove.

The guests wandered about under the venerable trees, sharing their memories of Carl, following the pathways he had marked out for them and in whose making many of them had shared. His chainsaw was unearthed from its hiding place under the roots of an ancient tree. At the end of the day, in a little ceremony of her own, Esther sprinkled some of her late husband's ashes about under the trees. "This is the place he loved the most," she said. "He thought this was heaven on earth, and this is where he'd want to be."

197

The bulk of his estate, about $48 million, he left to the Rollin M. Gerstacker Foundation.[12] He also specifically left the redwoods to the foundation as well. "I think he was afraid that if he left them to a family member they might get sold," said Alan Ott, the foundation's treasurer. "He wanted to be sure they'd be preserved, and not cut down for timber."

EPILOGUE

IT IS TOO EARLY TO MAKE AN ACCURATE ASSESSMENT OF Carl Gerstacker's imprint on history—that remains for future generations—but it is easy to speculate that he will go down as one of those legendary figures that speckle the pages of American business history, one of the industrial titans who built the foundations of America's greatness.

Even in his own lifetime it was difficult to sort out the stories of his exploits that were true, and those that had grown up as legends. In his early days as a financial guru he quickly became identified as springing out of the same mold as his mentor, Earl Bennett. In those days a company such as Dow, out in the hinterlands of America, would travel to Wall Street when it needed capital, and attempt to talk the nabobs of finance into providing what they needed, or part of it. Bennett and Gerstacker were both past masters at this art and similar in their approach—meek, unpretentious, scrupulously honest. That was not often a recipe for success on Wall Street.

Gerstacker told of an occasion when he traveled to New York by overnight train and as was his habit, left his shoes outside his Pullman berth to be shined by the porter during the long night trip. He carried a pair of old tennis shoes in his bag in lieu of slippers. On this occasion the train arrived in New York the next morning but his shoes had disappeared in the night and the porter said he had not seen them. There was nothing for Carl to do but go to his appointments wearing tennis shoes. Bennett had suffered a similar incident many years before, and thus grew up the legend of the country boys from Midland who went up to Wall Street in their tennis shoes to raise hundreds of millions of dollars.

Another oft-repeated story, also true, was that he once addressed an orientation class of new employees at Dow Chemical, as he loved to do, giving them fatherly advice about the careers upon which they were embarking. The best advice he could give them, he said, was to buy and accumulate Dow

stock as rapidly as they could. "You will never regret it," he told them. A hand went up in the audience. "When should we buy Dow stock?" an employee asked. "Whenever you have the money to buy some," Gerstacker said. Another hand went up. "When should we sell Dow stock?" He thought a moment. "I don't know the answer to that," he said. "I've never sold any."[1]

His sense of thrift was also legendary. He was one of the last, if not the last, top business executives to travel about the world commercial class, in the back of the plane. While other executives whizzed about in their private jets, or at the least in the first-class accommodations, he insisted on flying by the cheapest fare available, to set an example for his colleagues in the company. Once the editor of a New York financial magazine, who had been seeking a long, leisurely interview with him, proposed that they travel on the same flight from New York to Midland together, which would give them time for the interview. Gerstacker agreed to do so, but when the editor boarded the flight in first class he discovered his interviewee was nowhere to be seen; Gerstacker was in coach class in the back of the plane, and to the editor's chagrin they traveled to Midland separately. Gerstacker apologized, and made a date for the interview while the man was staying over in Midland.

He had a disreputable-looking green plastic raincoat that he carried with him to the ends of the earth. It became a kind of trademark. He had bought it for a few dollars at a K-Mart store, and he liked it because it was light—he always traveled light—and it folded up compactly in his bag. He would emerge from a long air flight wearing it, ready to face the elements.

He was "totally unimpressed by fashion," his stepdaughter Sandra Joys said. She remembered going to a "fat farm" with him in California. "He wouldn't ask you to do something he wouldn't do himself, so he went to the fat farm with us," she said. It was a high-toned and expensive place, attended mostly by rather wealthy folks from the eastern seaboard, she said,

and everyone enrolled had brand-new hiking shoes and chic new clothing to match, except Carl, who because they had told him there was a lot of hiking involved wore his old grungies and a pair of ancient Hush Puppies and carried his old green raincoat from K-Mart. "It didn't bother him in the least," she said.[2]

On one occasion he arrived in Venezuela to dedicate a big new Dow plastics plant, accompanied by Zoltan Merszei, who descended from the plane ahead of him looking fresh as a daisy and dressed to the nines. Gerstacker followed behind, wearing his dilapidated green raincoat. Waiting at the foot of the gangway was a TV crew from the Venezuelan national network, and they pounced on Merszei as he went by, thrust him in front of the cameras and began an interview. Merszei kept insisting he was not the person they wanted, while Gerstacker stood by watching the scene and smiling. Eventually, of course, it all got straightened out.

202

One of his hard-and-fast rules was that he did not express an opinion about something he knew nothing about. In the 1970s an X-rated movie house opened in Midland and immediately became the center of controversy. Daily it was the subject of letters to the editor of the newspaper. People copied down the license numbers of automobiles parked there, and sent them to the newspaper asking that they be published. Along with most of the population, Esther Gerstacker was terribly upset about it. She kept asking Carl for his opinion of the place. Carl said he did not have any, because he had never been there, and did not really know anything about that type of place. She pressed him to give his opinion anyway. Finally, he said, "If we're going to have an opinion it has to be based on fact, and the only way we can find out the facts is to go there ourselves." All the members of the family who wanted to see what the ruckus was about should go there in a group, he proposed.

So one evening Carl and Esther and two or three other family members went to the X-rated movie theater and marched down and sat in the front row, to see what it was. "We didn't stay very long after the film began," Sandra said, "but at least after that we had an informed opinion on the matter." The X-rated theater closed down after a few months for lack of customers, and has not reopened.

LEX

When he married Esther Schuette in 1975 Gerstacker also acquired, in addition to three stepchildren, four stepgrand-children—Bill and Jon Joys, the sons of Sandra, Esther's elder daughter, and Alexio and Dalhia Baum, the adopted children of Gretchen, Esther's younger daughter. Gretchen had married Dale Baum, of Midland, and they had adopted two babies, Alexio and Dalhia, who were African American, in 1972. Eventually the marriage soured and ended in divorce.[3]

"Carl's acceptance of Lex and Dalhia was total, warm, and fatherly," Gretchen said. "It was OK to talk about anything with Carl. He was so thoughtful about people and so understanding of their problems, and that was so sincere. There was never anything false about him.

"I remember," she said, "when I was going to divorce Dale, I talked to Carl about it, just to get his advice. It was a long conversation in the front of a car somewhere. He didn't tell me, 'Yes, you should divorce him,' or 'No, you shouldn't divorce him.' He just said, 'Well, keep in mind that you've got fifty more years to live, or more, and ask yourself if you want to spend it married to this man.'"[4]

Lex said that when he was five years old Carl gave him a golf club, and insisted he learn how to swing it. From time to time he gave him another club and instructions on swinging

203

it. "He couldn't drive nearly as far as I could," Lex said. "He beat you with his short game."

Lex' birthday was 4 August and Carl's was 6 August, and "for many years we never had separate birthdays," Lex said. Carl gave him lots of advice—"it was a grandfather-grandson relationship"—and he remembered Carl telling him, "You're going to make mistakes; we all do. What's important is how you deal with your mistakes, in what way. Don't run away from your mistake. Deal with it and move on."

"We were always friends of the best," Lex said. "With him it wasn't like having a relative, it was like having a friend."[5]

Carl's death left a vacancy on the board of the Gerstacker Foundation, and it fell to the Gerstacker "family" trustees to choose a successor. Their choice was Alexio Baum.

CHURCHMAN

His religion was a private matter with him, something he just did not talk about publicly. He instructed his speechwriter never to put the words "Jesus" or "Christ" in his talks. "I have an emotional reaction to them that I can't handle in a formal talk," he explained. He was an active participant in what were called "prayer breakfasts," events in which businessmen and politicians and public figures gathered and invoked divine guidance and blessings upon a new administration or undertaking. He was the master of ceremonies of these events on several occasions, including one sponsored by Gov. George Romney of Michigan and another starring Henry H. Fowler, who was then the secretary of the treasury.

He served as a Sunday school teacher for about ten years, and as an elder of his home church, Memorial Presbyterian, for six. Teaching Sunday school—fifth- and sixth-graders—was something he particularly enjoyed. He used the same basic

techniques in Sunday school as he used when guest teaching at grade schools or colleges. He taught a "basic business" course for two years at the Carpenter School in Midland, where the students made him a special honorary member of the class of 1989, and he was guest professor at Albion College and at other schools in the 1980s. He followed the same pattern he used at the dinner table at home. He always had a question for the young people at the table, and he would pose the question for discussion—usually one connected with current events. What would you do if you were X, who was in the news that day? Do you think X did the right thing, or the wrong thing, and why? He would ask everyone at the table, or in the Sunday school class, to give an opinion, and a reason for that opinion. Sometimes, but not always, he would take a vote, on what was the right thing or the wrong thing for the person in the news, or in the Sunday school lesson, to do.

"He always did his homework and was prepared" for his Sunday school lesson, observed Wally Mayton. "His preparation was usually a list of questions that he would throw out to the students about the lesson, and he would try to draw out all the members of the group and get them involved in the discussion. He always wanted to be a learner himself as well as the teacher. And it was truly extraordinary for a board chairman to be also a Sunday school teacher."[6]

His favorite hymn was "Amazing Grace," and sometimes he would sing it all by himself, driving down a lonely road. He insisted on an annual basis that it had to be played in some fashion the night before Thanksgiving. On one occasion, Sandra remembered, there was no music system in the house and in this emergency "he had our piano teacher play it for us over the phone on the eve of Thanksgiving." "'Amazing Grace' is often the favorite hymn of people who have a great deal of humility," Wally said. "Actually, the two best words to describe Carl Gerstacker are integrity—he was consistent in

doing always what he believed to be right, and humility—he was always willing to serve when the church asked him to take on a task, no matter how big it was, or how small."

He had what are called "high connections" in the Presbyterian Church, and was a friend of Howard Pew, of Philadelphia, one of the nation's leading philanthropists and chairman of the Presbyterian Foundation. Gerstacker was for some years the vice chairman of that fund. During the war in Vietnam and the worldwide protests against Dow's production of napalm, the Presbyterian Church decided to sell its holdings of Dow stock as a protest measure. Gerstacker was incensed.

"You have declared us guilty without hearing our side of the story," he told the church fathers. "What kind of shepherd attacks his own sheep? Not only is this wrong morally, it is wrong financially—Dow stock is historically one of the best investments you have had." He repeatedly asked the church to adopt a "realistic" stand when it opposed business, and at times he was almost a lone voice in the church pleading for more understanding of business. The Presbyterian Church appointed a task force to reconsider its relationship to the business world, and Gerstacker was a prominent member of this group.

It was a small victory for him when the church through its General Assembly adopted this task force's recommendations, which called for a much more understanding stance by the church of business, but he was disappointed that its overall attitude did not seem to change very much as a result.

LEGACY

Three former chief executives of the Dow company, asked individually about the legacy of Carl Gerstacker, were unanimous in their assessment. All three pointed to his impact on

the Dow company that he loved; his impact on Midland and the improvements he made to the city he loved; and the foundations he founded and nurtured—the Gerstacker, Pardee, and Midland Foundations.

"Carl's legacy is a company that is fundamentally sound and the requirement that there is never to be any compromise with anything that might have any other effect," said Frank Popoff in relation to the first of these. "He kept the character of the company solid, and if we remember him there will never be tradeoffs that could injure the character of the company. Dow will return time and again to its basic values and it must never compromise them. Dow must never get into a situation where it will be hostage to other people or interests. Nothing will be done by the company for the sake of expediency."[7]

Ted Doan agreed with this assessment. "Gerstacker had a total grip of Dow finances and everything involved in it," he added. "The innovations he made in finance he is not given enough credit for. Every finance guy at Dow, down to and including [Pedro] Reinhard [the current chief financial officer of Dow], has been better than the one before."[8]

"He was marvelously innovative as a financial officer," said Paul Oreffice, "and he tended to give Earl Bennett credit for all of it. The use of commercial paper was his idea, the matter of being listed [on the stock market] in Japan was something he supported strongly, the Dow Bank was extremely innovative and he was a strong supporter of it all the way. He was thinking ahead all the time. He was always two steps ahead of the crowd."

As chairman of the board, "he was the best," Oreffice said. "He was always probing for problems but he kept the meeting moving and on time. I learned most of what I know about being a board chairman from him."[9]

Oreffice recalled an incident that occurred when he was

at a meeting in the Detroit area with Earle Barnes, then president of Dow USA. The telephone rang and Barnes was called to the phone. "Earle picked it up and listened and listened and listened," Oreffice said. "When he was through he told me, 'I just got the biggest tongue-lashing of my life from Carl Gerstacker. He doesn't think we need a company jet and says there's no reason why with a little planning we can't all fly around commercial. He talked about the fall of the Roman empire happening for just that kind of reason.'" Later on, back in Midland, Gerstacker asked Oreffice if he was supportive of a company jet. Oreffice said he was because flying commercial was a stupid way to travel. "We're located in Midland, not in New York City," Oreffice told him. "We want and need to do things in a hurry, and we should." When they were through discussing it Gerstacker said, "Come with me." He and Oreffice walked down the hall to Ben Branch's office and Gerstacker said to Branch, "I want to be the person to propose to the board [of directors] that we buy a jet airplane. OK?" And so it was.

208

Ted Doan said Gerstacker was "extremely practical-minded. . . . He was the glue that kept me and Ben Branch from flying apart," he said, "and he was a doer. When he grabbed something and ran with it, it got done."

He and Carl became very close friends in spite of their rivalry for the Dow presidency. Ted remembered receiving a postcard from Caneel Bay, in the Virgin Islands, where Carl and Jayne were vacationing and trying to patch up their failing marriage. The card said simply, "Wish you were her," and the "her" was underlined.

Popoff observed that Gerstacker was the ultimate advocate of the stockholder at Dow. "For others," he said, "the top priority would be the employees—that was Ben Branch's top priority, for instance. But for Carl Gerstacker it was always the Dow stockholder who was the first consideration."

"Gerstacker was always synonymous with community and interest in the well-being of the community," Popoff said in relation to his contributions to Midland, "but it was hard to get a check out of him. He felt Dow employees were well-paid and owed something back to their community, and that the initiative and much of the backing for community improvements should come from them. When Main Street was redone he led the way in persuading the company that it was to its advantage to do these things. There was a lot of opposition to Dow putting money into the building of a downtown hotel and conference center but Gerstacker saw it as an investment. "We're a world class company and we need a world-class town," he contended.

Gerstacker will long be remembered as Dow's "symbol and leader of frugality," Popoff said. "He was the source of the Dow dictum against ruffles and flourishes, against spending unwisely—the prime advocate of frugality at Dow." This extended to a steadfast opposition to the purchase of technology from other companies.

Once, Popoff said, Dow bought some phenol technology from Allied Chemical. Gerstacker opposed it, saying that Dow, the world's largest producer of phenol, should not be buying someone else's technology. "The idea of such a thing makes me want to throw up on the carpet," Gerstacker said.

He was also the voice of reason, Popoff said. "For a long time people like Branch and L. I. Doan were saying 'Rah, rah' for geographical expansion. The mantra was 'let's do what we've always done well, but do it all over the world.' Gerstacker wanted Dow to expand into new businesses rather than geographically. He for example got involved with Hartford Insurance, which was way out of Dow's field."

At board meetings Gerstacker always asked the "what if" questions, Popoff said. "No one was better at it. He was always aiming at getting us [the Dow board] to reach a consensus."

Once Gerstacker was gone, Popoff said, the board members would often ask themselves, "What would Gerstacker say?" when an issue was brought before them. This was particularly true in relation to dividend policy, and in relation to acquisitions that might be dilutive of the value to stockholders.

Oreffice, for whom Gerstacker was "my hero," also remembered what a terrible loser he was at a great variety of sports. "At gin rummy," Oreffice remarked, "he was the worst loser in history. On one occasion the two of us went on an extended tour of Latin America, and in the off-hours and waiting in airports we played a running game of gin. I was ahead all the way, and on the last night of the trip Carl tried desperately to catch up to me, and we played all night, and I still came out ahead. But my hero didn't pay me, and I was very puzzled, because he always paid his debts promptly. Then a letter arrived from Carl. 'I tried my best,' he wrote, 'but you're a better gin rummy player than I am. Check is enclosed.'"

210

Table tennis, or Ping-Pong, was one of the sports Carl was very good at, and considered himself very good, Oreffice said. One evening he and Carl got into a match and Oreffice beat him game after game, probably eight games in a row. All the games were close, but Oreffice won them all. Gerstacker got very upset about it. "You're holding back,' he told Oreffice, "you're not playing your best. I want to beat you when you're playing your best."

Ted Doan remembered the intense rivalry between Gerstacker and Branch, "with me in the middle all the time." Ben Branch would say, "I'm going to build more plants than you can ever finance." Gerstacker would respond, "You can't build more plants than I can finance."

In the end it was the company that came out ahead, and the city of Midland, and the world's cancer victims, and

universities and charitable organizations the world over that benefited from the grants made by the foundations he established.

NAMING OPPORTUNITIES

In the world of philanthropy they are called "naming opportunities"—i.e., if a donor or a foundation makes a substantial gift to an organization the building or program being financed will be named for the donor as he or she may wish.

During his philanthropic career Gerstacker received constant offers to name things the Carl A. Gerstacker Building, or Stadium, or Field, or Professorship, or whatever, in return for a substantial contribution of money—and all such offers he turned down. He rejected proposals of this kind regularly and routinely. There were a few rare exceptions when places were named in his honor by some board over which he had no control or after a gift had been made. For example, the Carl A. Gerstacker Building at the Midland County Fairgrounds is named in honor of his many contributions and gifts to the fair over the course of his lifetime.

Now that he is not around to oppose such things, his name has begun appearing in all kinds of places. In 1995, for example, the Midland Chamber of Commerce decided to call its new headquarters building the Carl A. Gerstacker Business Center. Hiram College in 2002 inaugurated the Carl and Esther Gerstacker Science Building. Buildings and scholarships and professorships and chairs are already named for him at the University of Michigan, Albion College, Saginaw Valley State University, Delta College, Northwood University, and a host of other institutions.

One of his favorites would certainly have been the Carl A. Gerstacker Nature Preserve, which is situated on the southern

211

shore of Michigan's Upper Peninsula, a few miles east of Cedarville. It is home to such rare and endangered species as the dwarf iris and Pitcher's thistle, and is watched over by the Nature Conservancy, which owns it. The territory was purchased with contributions made in his memory by a half-dozen of Midland's leading foundations and firms. He had been the first treasurer of the Nature Conservancy organization when it established a Michigan chapter, many years before.

It is probably only the beginning. In the years ahead, how many more organizations, inspired by the example and help of a Carl Gerstacker, may be moved to name something in his memory or honor? Who knows what the future holds?

APPENDIX

ORAL HISTORY INTERVIEWS
(Interviewee, date, location, interviewer[s])

Ballman, Donald K., 23 September 1988, La Jolla, California (James J. Bohning).

Barnes, Earle B., 22 October 1988, Freeport, Texas and 11 November 1988, Grand Rapids, Michigan (James J. Bohning).

Bennett, Earl W., 1962, Midland, Michigan (Clarence E. [Dusty] Rhodes).

Bennett, Robert B., 24 August 1990, Midland, Michigan (James J. Bohning and E. N. Brandt).

Beutel, Albert P. (Dutch), 1967, Freeport, Texas (Don Whitehead).

Boundy, Ray H., 9 September 1988, Midland, Michigan (James J. Bohning).

Branch, C. Benson (Ben), 12 November 1988, Houston, Texas (James J. Bohning), and 8–9 March 1996, Houston (Holmes H. McClure).

Butler, Andrew J., 5 May 1995, Midland, Michigan (James J. Bohning and E. N. Brandt).

Doan, Herbert D., 29 July 1988, 2 August 1988, and 17 January 1989, Midland, Michigan (James J. Bohning and Arnold Thackray) and 3 November 1989, Midland, Michigan (Judith O'Dell).

Fassler, Edmund P., 7 July 1989, Zurich, Switzerland (James J. Bohning and E. N. Brandt).

Gerstacker, Carl A., 21 July 1988, Midland, Michigan (James J. Bohning).

Gerstacker, Esther Schuette, 29 April 1991 (E. N. Brandt).

Johnson, Julius E., 9 September 1988, Midland, Michigan (Terry S. Reynolds).

Keil, Robert M., 8 August 1990, Midland, Michigan (James J. Bohning and E. N. Brandt).

Look, Alfred T. (Al), 2 October 1990, Canyon Lake, Texas (James J. Bohning and E. N. Brandt).

Lundeen, Robert W., 14 October 1988, Midland, Michigan (Reynolds).

Lyon, Herbert H., 7 August 1990, Midland, Michigan (James J. Bohning and E. N. Brandt).

McKennon, Keith R., 9 June 1993, Midland, Michigan (E. N. Brandt).

Merszei, Zoltan, 21 December 1988 and 3 April 1989, Greenwich, Connecticut and 3 June 1994, New York City (James J. Bohning).

Naegele, Robert E., 6 August 1990, Midland, Michigan (James J. Bohning and E. N. Brandt).

Oreffice, Paul F., 1 August 1988, Midland, Michigan (James J. Bohning).

Popoff, Frank P., 16 November 1995, Midland, Michigan (E. N. Brandt and Arnold Thackray).

Rooke, David L., 3 October 1990, Kerrville, Texas (E. N. Brandt and James J. Bohning).

Temple, Joseph G. Jr., 28 October 1988, Midland, Michigan (James J. Bohning) and 9 October 1995, Midland, Michigan (James J. Bohning and E. N. Brandt).

Whiting, Macauley, 13 August 1990, Midland, Michigan (James J. Bohning and E. N. Brandt).

Williams, G. James, 16 August 1990, Midland, Michigan (James J. Bohning and E. N. Brandt).

NOTES

CHAPTER 1

1. Letter to parents, 23 April 1941.
2. Oral history Carl A. Gerstacker [hereinafter referred to as OHCAG], 21 July 1988, 7–8. Much of the material in this chapter is taken from this source.
3. "Present wife" refers to Gerstacker's second wife, Esther Schuette Gerstacker, whose "only male son," at that time a U.S. Congressman from Michigan, is William D. Schuette, Gerstacker's stepson.
4. OHCAG, 17–18.
5. Carl Gerstacker, "The Industrialist's Voice," speech to General Federation of Women's Clubs, Denver, 9 June 1972.
6. Carl Gerstacker, "Two Wars and Two Debts," high school commencement address as salutatorian, Cleveland, January 1934.

CHAPTER 2

1. Letter to parents, 21 February 1934. Gerstacker contended jokingly that he was "an illegal" when he was hired at Dow because he was not yet eighteen, the legal age for employment.
2. Letter to parents, 29 April 1934.
3. OHCAG, 19, 20.
4. Ibid., 15, 16.
5. Letter to parents, 1935, dated only "Sunday."
6. Letter to parents, 1936, dated only "Thursday."
7. Letter to parents, 1936, undated, labeled "letter home."
8. Letter to parents, 1937, dated only "Sunday."
9. OHCAG, 21, 22.
10. Ibid., 23.
11. Ibid., 24.
12. Ibid., 22.

CHAPTER 3

1. The U.S. Congress had authorized the call-up, for one year of

service, of officers needed to aid the nation's allies, and Gerstacker was called up under this provision.

2. OHCAG, 26
3. Letter to parents, 9 March 1941.
4. Letter to parents, 12 October 1941.
5. Letter to parents, 26 October 1941.
6. Letter to parents, 18 February 1942.
7. Intraoffice Memorandum, Detroit Ordnance District, 21 May 1942.
8. Letter to parents, 7 June 1942.
9. Letter to parents, 22 August 1942.
10. Letter to parents, 13 June 1943.
11. Letter to parents, 25 September 1943.
12. Letter to parents, 27 November 1943.
13. Letter to parents, 11 December 1943.
14. Letter to parents, 18 January 1945.
15. Letter to parents, 14 September 1944.
16. Letter to parents, 6 February 1945.
17. Letter to parents, 18 January 1945.
18. Letter to mother, 9 May 1945.
19. Letter to mother, 8 July 1945.
20. OHCAG, 28.

CHAPTER 4

1. Years later, Gerstacker was "elected" to fire Milt LeFevre from Dow, a story he relates in his oral history. LeFevre was extremely angry at the time, but six months later he asked to see Gerstacker and told him it was the best thing that had ever happened to him. He had established his own business, loved it, and was successful at it. The two men remained close friends the rest of their lives.
2. *Annual Report,* Dow Chemical Company, 1948.
3. The others named to the Dow board of directors at this time were Albert P. Beutel, Nelson D. Griswold (Beutel's principal

lieutenant), Calvin A. Campbell, and Russell L. Curtis (general manager of Dow's Western Division).

4. "H. D. Doan New Dow President," Gerstacker quoted in *Saginaw News,* 13 September 1962.

5. Letter to mother from Wyomissing, Pennsylvania, 3 January 1943.

6. "Jayne Cunningham, Carl Gerstacker Wed," *Midland Daily News,* 24 October 1950.

7. The Dow Chemical Company was founded in Cleveland in 1897, and its board of directors in the early years consisted almost entirely of Cleveland-area businessmen and academics. The monthly meeting of the board was held in Cleveland until 1918.

8. Gerstacker, untitled talk to Dow employees, 20 February 1975.

9. OHCAG, 37–38.

10. "68-Year Chronology of Dow Chemical Company," *Midland Daily News,* 1 May 1958.

11. "Dow's Foreign Empire—Gerstacker Sees It Getting Even Bigger, but at a Slower Pace," *Saginaw News,* 27 April 1975.

12. "Mrs. W. W. Allen's Funeral Is Tuesday," *Midland Daily News,* 9 March 1957; editorial, "Mrs. Elsa Allen Was Interested in Midland," *Midland Daily News,* 11 March 1957.

13. Citation conferring honorary Doctor of Laws degree on Carl Allan Gerstacker, C. L. Anspach, president, Central Michigan College, Mt. Pleasant, Michigan, 9 June 1957.

14. Rollin M. Gerstacker Foundation, income statement, 12 months ended 25 December 1957.

15. See E. N. Brandt, *Growth Company: Dow Chemical's First Century* (East Lansing: Michigan State University Press, 1997), 299–301.

CHAPTER 5

1. See "Youth Takes Over in Business and Government," *U.S. News & World Report,* 5 December 1960.

2. H. D. Doan, oral history, Midland, Michigan, 29 July 1988, 2 August 1988, 17 July 1989.

3. OHCAG, 46.

4. P. F. Oreffice, interview by author, 31 May 2002.

5. C. B. Branch, oral history, Houston, 12 November 1988.

6. "Honor Bennett at Testimonial," *Midland Daily News,* 19 January 1960.

7. "Governor, Doan Exchange Kudos," *Midland Daily News,* 10 November 1964.

8. "A Salute," *Midland Daily News,* 8 February 1967.

9. "Industry Can Afford Pollution Control, Gerstacker Claims," *Midland Daily News,* 24 March 1966; "Industry, Cities Challenged in Pollution Battle," *Bay City Times,* 24 March 1966; "Industry Gets Pollution Challenge—Use Imagination, Dow Leader Says," *Saginaw Daily News,* 24 March 1966.

10. Carl Gerstacker, "Profits and Pollution," speech to Economic Club of Detroit, 22 February 1972.

11. Emanuel Doernberg, "Gerstacker Sets Sights High for Dow Chemical," *N.Y. American,* 11 December 1960.

12. "Lessons of Leadership, Part LXXIV, Carl Gerstacker of Dow Chemical Co.," *Nation's Business,* July 1971.

13. "Saline Water Plant Gets VIP Sendoff," *Chemical & Engineering News,* 3 July 1961.

14. Macauley Whiting, oral history, Midland, Michigan, 13 August 1990.

15. Carl Gerstacker, "The New Role of Top Management," speech to Global Dow meeting, 16–18 March 1965, Michigan State University, East Lansing, Mich.; Gerstacker, untitled talk, management meetings, 16–18 March 1965.

16. "Gerstacker Urges Increased Exports to Halt Dollar Drain," *International Trade News,* published by International Trade Club of Chicago, November 1966. See also multiple speeches on this subject in Speeches 00455A–00455J A. J. Gerstacker, Post St. Archives.

17. Carl A. Gerstacker, Certificate of Appreciation, U.S. Dept. of Commerce, 13 December 1973.

18. Gen. Earle G. Wheeler, chairman of Joint Chiefs of Staff, statement on use of napalm in Vietnam, 27 February 1967.

19. Doan, oral history.

20. See Howard A. Rusk, M.D., "Vietnam Tour–I, Reports of Many Children Burned By American Napalm Are Challenged," *New York Times,* 12 March 1967; Howard A. Rusk, M.D., "Vietnam Medicine–I, Visiting American Team, on Its Return, Reports to Johnson on Napalm Burns," *New York Times,* 1 October 1967; "A Doctor Looks at Vietnam," *Dow Diamond* 31, no. 4 (1968).

21. OHCAG, 55–58.

22. Carl Gerstacker, "Living with Confrontation," speech to New York Financial Writers, New York City, 3 June 1970.

23. Greg Helmling, "Midland's Been Good to Gerstacker—and Vice Versa," *Midland Daily News,* 11 March 1989; Paul Rau, "Carl A. Gerstacker: Never a President, Always a Principal," *Saginaw News,* in the *Midland Daily News,* 18 May 1997.

24. Bette M. Gerstacker, interview by author, 21 May 2002.

25. Jean Worth, "Dow Chairman Favors Treaty with Russia," *Mt. Pleasant (Mich.) Times-News,* 9 February 1967; Jean Worth, "Dow Chief Is For Ties with Russia," *Escanaba (Mich.) Daily Press,* 9 February 1967.

CHAPTER 6

1. Bette M. Gerstacker, interview; Lisa J. Gerstacker, interview by author, 28 February 2002.

2. John B. Scofield, M.D., "Why Kids Rebel," *Parents' Magazine,* June 1963.

3. Bette M. Gerstacker, interview.

4. Lisa J. Gerstacker, interview.

5. A. T. Look, oral history, Canyon Lake, Texas, 2 October 1990.

6. "Nixon on Future Anti-Inflation Policy: 'Selective Controls

with Teeth,'" *Midland Daily News,* 24 September 1971; "Liked Nixon's Answers, Gerstacker says," *Midland Daily News,* 24 September 1971.

7. See letter to parents, 26 October 1941.

8. Yoshizane Iwasa, chairman, Fuji Bank, Ltd., Tokyo, letter to Gerstacker, 26 November 1973; Mitsuo Mutai, president, *Yomiuri Shimbun,* Tokyo, letter to Gerstacker, 26 November 1973.

9. Carl Gerstacker, letter to Iwasa, 4 December 1973; Carl Gerstacker, letter to Mutai, 4 December 1973.

10. Carl Gerstacker, address to Fourth Symposium on International Economic and Business Cooperation, Tokyo, 16 April 1974.

11. Esther Schuette Gerstacker, oral history, 29 April 1991. Much of this section is based on this oral history and on an interview with Esther S. Gerstacker, 20 June 2002.

12. Gerstacker's peculiar eating habits at least once put him in an embarrassing situation. At a state dinner in the Gerald Ford White House he was cutting his meat with his fork one evening, as was his custom, when the fork, made of gold, folded over. "What do you do," Gerstacker asked, "when you're at the White House eating with a gold fork that folds up on you? Hide it under the napkin? Call a waiter and ask for a new one? Drop it under your chair?" As it happened, an alert waiter saw what had occurred and quickly rescued him.

13. For a fuller and more detailed account of this selection process, see "Zoltan," chap. 17, in Brandt, *Growth Company,* which is based in large part on the notes Gerstacker kept of these meetings.

14. See "Dow Press Analysis, No. 72," Public Relations Dept., Dow Chemical Company, 14 June 1976.

15. Carl Gerstacker, "A Look at the Record—Dow, 1950–1975," speech at Annual Meeting of Shareholders, Dow, 5 May 1976.

CHAPTER 7

1. "Luncheon for Former Chairman, The Dow Chemical Co. and Mrs. Carl A. Gerstacker," *America-Japan Society Bulletin* (16 June 1976): 4–6.
2. Esther S. Gerstacker, oral history and interview.
3. Greg Helmling, "Gerstacker Has His 'Day' at Albion," *Midland Daily News,* 18 April 1988.
4. Melvin L. Vulgamore, president, Albion College, "Endowment and Naming of the Carl A. Gerstacker Liberal Arts Program in Professional Management," memorandum to faculty and staff, 6 April 1988. See also related materials, Albion College archives.
5. For a fuller account of the "seven days in May," see Brandt, *Growth Company,* 501–18.
6. "A Swashbuckler Tries His Talents at Oxy," *Business Week,* 29 October 1979, 176.
7. Robert B. Bennett, oral history, Midland, Michigan, 24 August 1990.
8. John Van Stirum, "Why Dow Got Into the Money Game," interview, *Burroughs Clearing House,* publication of Burroughs Corp., December 1968.
9. Edmund P. Fassler, oral history, Zurich, Switzerland, 7 July 1989.
10. Dow Banking Corp., Zurich, circular letter, August 1986.
11. John H. Bryan Jr., chairman and CEO, Sara Lee Corp., interview, *Directors & Boards* (spring 2001).
12. Robert M. Keil, oral history, Midland, Michigan, 8 August 1990.
13. R. M. Keil to E. C. Yehle, 21 March 1983.

CHAPTER 8

1. Carl Gerstacker, untitled talk to United Cancer Council meeting at Midland, 22 October 1981.
2. Annual report, the Elsa U. Pardee Foundation, 2000.

3. See *Rollin M. Gerstacker Foundation: 45 Years of Giving* (Midland, Mich.: Rollin M. Gerstacker Foundation, June 2002).

4. F. P. Popoff, interview by author, 17 September 2002.

5. In his will, for instance, James Pardee left a bequest to the State of Michigan "to be used for the benefit of handicapped children." The state had no suitable fund for the bequest at the time and the money lay idle for years, in the meantime accumulating because it was invested in Dow Chemical common stock. Eventually the bequest became the basis of a state fund for Children with Special Problems, and Michigan residents today are asked whether they wish to contribute to this fund as part of their state income tax return.

6. In the event both Carl and Esther Gerstacker were out of town or unavailable, the author was also authorized to approve Barley MacTavish grants.

7. John Zimmerman, executive director of United Way of Midland County, interview by author, 24 October 2002.

8. Esther Schuette Gerstacker, oral history and interview.

225

CHAPTER 9

1. Keith Naughton, "Execs Need Heed Power-less Pitfalls—Successful Retirees Must 'Re-dream and Renew Themselves,' Analysts Say," *Detroit News*, 26 February 1990.

2. Carl and Esther Gerstacker, videotaped interview by Philip Mason for Council of Michigan Foundations, Wayne State University, 1991.

3. "Tridge Unites Midland," in brochure, *45 Years of Giving*, Rollin M. Gerstacker Foundation, June 2002.

4. Ted O'Neil, "Law Enforcement Community Turns Tables on Gerstackers," *Midland Daily News*, February 1993.

5. William D. Schuette, interview by author, 16 September 2002.

6. Rev. Wallace H. Mayton III, interview by author, 22 August 2002.

7. Carl Allan Gerstacker Death Certificate, State of Michigan,

Dept. of Public Health, 23 April 1995.

8. Resolution, Board of Directors, Dow Chemical Company, 11 May 1995.

9. Sixteenth Amendment to the Carl A. Gerstacker Revocable Trust, Estate of Carl A. Gerstacker Deceased, Form 706, U.S. Estate Tax Return, 4–5.

10. William D. Schuette, interview.

11. Records of the "celebration in the redwoods," including invitation list, attendance, etc., supplied by Sandra Schuette Joys.

12. Estate of Carl A. Gerstacker Deceased, Form 706, U.S. Estate Tax Return

EPILOGUE

1. Popoff, interview.

2. Sandra Schuette Joys, interview by author, 20 August 2002.

3. To make the family relationships more complicated, it should be noted that Dale Baum was the son of Bobbe Baum Allen by her first husband. She became the second wife of William W. Allen after the death of Elsa Gerstacker, Carl's sister.

4. Gretchen Schuette, interview by author, 9 August 2002.

5. Alexio R. Baum, interview by author, 6 September 2002.

6. Mayton, interview.

7. Popoff, interview.

8. H. D. Doan, interview by author, 21 June 2002.

9. Paul F. Oreffice, interview by author, 31 May 2002.

INDEX

229

231

236

238

CHAIRMAN OF THE BOARD